REAL
HARD
CASES

Also by Robert Jeffrey:

Crimes Past – Glasgow's Crimes of the Century
Glasgow Crimefighter (with Les Brown)
Blood on the Streets
Glasgow's Godfather
Gangland Glasgow
Glasgow's Hard Men
The Wee Book of Glasgow
The Wee Book of the Clyde

*

Images of Glasgow
Scotland's Sporting Heroes
The Herald Book of the Clyde
Doon the Watter
Clydeside, People and Places
(all with Ian Watson)

LES BROWN &
ROBERT JEFFREY

REAL
HARD
CASES

UNSOLVED CRIMES REINVESTIGATED

Black & White Publishing

First published 2006
by Black & White Publishing Ltd
99 Giles Street, Edinburgh, EH6 6BZ

ISBN 13: 978 1 84502 122 1
ISBN 10: 1 84502 122 3

A CIP catalogue record for this book is available from
The British Library.

Printed and bound by Creative Print and Design Group Ltd

This book is dedicated to:

Moira Anderson
Annie Davies
Innes Ewart
Jacqueline Gallagher
Pamela Hastie
John Kidd
Renee and Andrew MacRae
Kevin McLeod
Tracey Waters
Ann Whittle
Sadie Young

CONTENTS

Introduction

Once a detective, always a detective. The buzz of an investigation never goes away. A mystery is hard to resist, an unsolved mystery even more so. After twenty-six years in Strathclyde Police, mostly dealing with murders on the streets of this violent city, I retired from the force. There followed seventeen years working for the Federation Against Copyright Theft. The mysteries I encountered in this work may have been less bloody but they were often just as intriguing and it was certainly more entertaining trying to curb video pirates and the like than it was hunting down axe murderers and perverts.

Once this second strand to my career as an investigator ended, it was not long before I was back in the thick of violent death and unsolved mysteries. The tabloids always have close links with what is going on in the streets and, when the *Sunday Mail* highlighted the death of Annie Davies of Erskine in May 1998 in a series of features on this unsolved case, they turned to me – four years later – for help. As part of their ongoing examination of the case, one of their top reporters, Marion Scott, asked me to visit old Annie's family to see if I could help in a mystery surrounding her death – murder or accident? – which seemed to be defeating the police. The publicity surrounding all this resulted in the forming of an organisation called A Search for Justice. Initially, it was started by me and Annie's son Bryan who was relentlessly pursuing the mysteries surrounding his mother's death. Others who felt they had been ill served by the police or other investigators soon joined A Search for Justice. A professional computer consultant was brought on board and grateful relatives of the victims of crime donated money to finance the work. We had a big caseload though some requests were politely declined – like the case of a Bearsden man who wanted help in a battle with his neighbours over the height of a hedge. 'We don't do hedges,' he was told.

But, in early 2006, came trouble. I took it upon myself to agree to help the staff of the Scottish Criminal Records Office in their fight for what they saw as justice in the controversial Shirley McKie fingerprints case. This did not please Bryan Davies and the others in the organisation and a decision was taken to disband it. I learned of this on the organisation's website. I have not spoken to Bryan Davies since that day. Sadly, an organisation dedicated to helping victims of injustice had been swept away. But this book tells some of the intriguing stories I investigated for the group and covers many other mysteries from my long and satisfying career as a detective.

Some of these tales are critical of the police but the reader should be aware that there are a million reported crimes every year in Scotland and, as in every walk of life, things can go wrong on occasion.

Les Brown

1

FATAL FALLS AND POLICE FLAWS

High on the list of scenarios for the perfect murder is death by falling from a high place. 'Did he fall or was he pushed?' is no joke. Some of the most difficult crime investigations have centred on incidents on mountaintops. When two people are in a high, dangerous place, there are no witnesses on a bleak windswept mountain and not a CCTV camera for miles around. If someone falls to his or her death, who is to know if it was a slip made by a perhaps inexperienced mountaineer or if the fatal plunge came after a gentle nudge by an enemy?

And it is not necessary to fall thousands of feet to die or even to slip off a cliff. In my 'search for justice', I came on two truly puzzling cases in which the victims did not fall too far but it was far enough for them to die. Both involved young men from the north of Scotland. Both appear to show that the police investigations, from as far apart as Wick and London, were sadly lacking in commitment. And they also show, to my mind, the classic error in an investigation of making up your mind too quickly and accepting a convenient explanation for facts that are much more complex than they might appear at the moment of the discovery of a death.

The first of these mysteries concerns the fate of twenty-seven-year-old Innes Ewart, a personable young man from Inverness brought up by loving parents in that most pleasant of areas. He was found dead on a pavement adjacent to a car park several storeys high in Stratford, East London, on 21 January 2001, not far from what will be the site of the 2012 Olympics.

He was only supposed to be passing through London that tragic weekend. Innes was intelligent and well educated with many friends in Scotland and abroad. Like many of today's youngsters, his field was information technology and he worked in the industry for a computer outfit in Munich. He was undoubtedly good at the job and he was held in high esteem by his employers and colleagues. But, like a lot of young folk, he may have been a tad impetuous and, at short notice, on 19 January, he suddenly decided to leave Germany and return home. A good-looking young fellow, he had a girlfriend in Germany and perhaps one of the reasons he decided to go home was that they had fallen out. Alternatively, he could simply have been homesick and, working in an industry where it is relatively easy to switch jobs, he just chose to head home to Scotland.

At any rate, with his mind made up, he acted decisively. He handed in his notice, cleared out his flat and withdrew 3000 marks from his bank account. He travelled to London with the intention of catching the overnight sleeper north to the Highlands. He then discovered that the sleeper did not run on the Saturday night. So he changed his plans, intending to stay in

London that night and take the train on the Sunday night. It was a move that was to cost him his life. On arrival at Euston, he left his suitcase in the left luggage there.

By this time, he had converted his German marks into sterling – around £1000 – and, with the cash in his wallet and carrying a holdall filled with computer programmes that represented his life's work, he then did something that remains unexplained – he travelled to Stratford in the East End. It is an old joke that tourists in London see Stratford on the destination board of a red bus and assume that it is going to the birthplace of William Shakespeare. But Innes Ewart was clearly not that naive. Maybe he was en route to a look up an old friend or maybe he had just seen a film that he wanted to see advertised as showing at a cinema there. Maybe he felt it would be better to go the cinema there than in the expensive West End. Whatever the reason for the so-far unexplained journey, he arrived in Stratford around half past two in the afternoon and bought a ticket in a multi-screen for a film that was due to start in ten minutes' time. He never saw it. A few minutes after he had bought the ticket, two men unloading a delivery van nearby, at the rear of some shops, heard a thud and saw the body of Innes lying on the ground a few yards from them. His personal belongings were not with him – the £1000 in cash was gone as was the holdall with the IT material that was so valuable to him. There was also no sign of an expensive Raymond Weil wristwatch his mother Pat had given him as a Christmas present. The police were alerted and an officer travelled in the ambulance taking Innes to the hospital.

The immediate assumption of the London cops was that Innes had thrown himself off the roof of the car park and his mum and dad were informed by the police in Inverness that their son had committed suicide. Right from the start, this was strange. You don't need to have been in the police force for very long when you realise that suicide jumpers tend to choose really tall buildings to jump from. They will do so to ensure that they die rather than risk survival and the painful injuries that throwing themselves from more modest heights might result in.

So it is little wonder that, 600 or so miles away from the scene of their son's death, Ron and Pat Ewart could not believe what they were hearing. The incident, in their view, had not been properly investigated and countless pleas to the authorities to conduct a more thorough investigation went unheeded. They turned to me as the co-founder of A Search for Justice and someone known to be interested in taking up unsolved 'hard cases' for help. I travelled north where, naturally, I found Innes's parents distraught. It is always difficult to cope with such shocking news, especially when it is delivered on your doorstep out of the blue. I was immediately struck by this likeable couple's totally unshakable conviction that their son would not and did not take his own life. They were sure he was not on medication or depressed. At that first meeting, they convinced me Innes would not have committed suicide and, in the years since, I have continued to believe, as they do, that this was no suicide.

I made myself as aware of the details of the case as I could. I then contacted Stratford police and I was put through to a senior female police officer who, on listening to me introduce myself and my interest, said, 'Yes, the boy who jumped off the roof of the car park.' I did not like this one bit and, after some argy-bargy, I asked if there was a Scottish police officer available to talk to me. I was put through to a guy who was originally from Coatbridge – progress. He confirmed that the consensus of opinion in the local CID was that Innes had committed suicide. I said to him, 'If you can tell me what happened to his watch, I'll hang up and that's the last you'll hear from me.' He couldn't and I didn't.

I made the obvious points. Why would a person bent on killing himself buy a cinema ticket minutes before his death? Why would he jump from a roof that wasn't particularly high? Why was there no money on the body minutes after he'd paid for his ticket? I got no satisfactory answers.

I thought long and hard about the perplexing facts before coming up with, to my mind, a more realistic scenario than that swallowed by the London cops. I figured that, after he had bought the ticket, Innes must have stepped outside the cinema for a moment and been mugged. Muggings are not in the least unusual in this area. One man, or perhaps two, armed with a knife or firearm, could have spotted the holdall and taken it and the money and the watch. My training as a detective and my instinct make me believe the mugger(s) may have been watching the cinema queue looking for suitable targets. The flashy watch may have caught their eye and perhaps Innes's accent convinced them that here was an out-of-towner ripe for attack. It is common for folk attacked in this way to try anything to get their property back. Innes could have run after his assailants to try at least to snatch the holdall with his valuable computer programmes back. Muggers like a quick getaway and perhaps they had left a car on the roof of the car park and Innes could have caught up with them there. I believe this is what happened and, when he challenged them, the muggers then threw Innes from the roof.

I told my theory to the London detective and said that it would suggest that such attacks were far from rare in the area. I was staggered on the reply – 'In a good week, we get fifty such robberies and, in a bad week, we can get eighty.' My next question was obvious – 'Is all this consistent with my theory of what happened to Innes?' 'Very much so,' was the answer. Incidentally I later discovered that the late Tony Banks, former Sports Minister, had been the victim of a similar attack – and he was the MP for the area.

At a Coroner's Inquest in Walthamstow in August 2001, an open verdict was recorded. After numerous meetings with Innes's, parents, we decided to try to enlist the help of the TV programme *Crimewatch UK*. In particular, we thought the exposure might help to trace the distinctive watch but, unfortunately, we never ended up on the programme. Inverness MP David Stewart helped in the search for new evidence and he even spoke to the Home Secretaries David Blunkett and Charles Clarke about it.

There was, however, another line of inquiry. I had been shown photographs of the area and it was obvious that there were CCTV cameras galore in the area of the cinema and the adjoining streets. The car park had cameras covering entrance and exit and one of them had caught Innes leaving the lift area for the top floor of the car park. The image showed that he was not carrying anything. One of the police officers attending the death scene spoke to the assistant manager of the cinema who confirmed that the camera covering the premises' entrance was operating. He assumed the police would take it but they did not.

The years of anguish continued for Innes's parents and, in October 2005, a divisional commander travelled all the way from London to talk to them but his visit did not really shed any light on the situation. As a former serving detective, I find such a visit odd – could this have been the London police showing signs of a collective guilty conscience?

The Ewarts have not given up trying to find out what happened to their son and they are hoping a second inquest will be held. In July 2006, Mrs Ewart told the *Sunday Post* that they had spoken to lawyers in England about such a move which the Attorney General could grant if he feels 'there has been a lack of investigation'. She said that it is a last resort and, even if it didn't provide all the answers, 'it could point the finger at those who didn't do their job'. At the original inquest the coroner, Dr Elizabeth Stearns, said she returned an open verdict because she was not satisfied that Innes killed himself, albeit that there was no evidence of third party involvement. In her view:

[T]he police may have concluded that the death was not suspicious but they should not state that Innes killed himself. I believe the evidence has not fully disclosed how Innes came by his death. I would support any measure which might shed further light on the death.

David Stewart MP has fought hard for the Ewarts, a pleasant well-to-do couple with a successful business background. The MP says there has been a serious miscarriage of justice. I agree and I think anyone who has looked at the story will too – except perhaps the Met. That police force, which closed the case a few short hours after the finding of the body, said of the request for a second inquest:

> The death was investigated and a full report sub-mitted to the coroner. An inquest recorded an open verdict. There are no further active lines of inquiry. However, we would support anything the family seek to achieve regarding further information.

In my view, a proper investigation back in 2001 would have solved the problem.

The mysterious of the death of Innes Ewart was played out in the grubby streets of London's violent East End. Some four years earlier, in far different surroundings, an equally puzzling death occurred, again after a fall. This time the scene was the picturesque harbour of Wick in far north Scotland, a place that attracts tourists to stroll around breathing the fresh air whistling in off the cold North Sea. It is not the sort of place you expect to find a mystery of the did-he-fall-or-was-he-pushed? variety. Yet the unexplained death of twenty-five-year-old electrician Kevin McLeod is a classic of the kind.

Kevin had been born and raised in the fishing town, the oldest of three sons of Hugh McLeod and his wife June. He left school at fifteen and served his time as an electrician and, at the time of his death, he was working with a company called Rockwater at Wester.

In view of what happened to poor Kevin it is important to say right away that his family were adamant that he was a good son and known for his good behaviour. In particular they say that they had never seen him under the influence of drink. A great passion in life was his car, a speedy Ford Sierra Cosworth, which he lavished much time on, keeping it well fettled and using it mainly at weekends. He had a fiancée, Emma, who worked in the town as a nurse. They had planned to marry on 30 May 1997. They had been allocated a council house in Wick and, in time-honoured fashion, they spent time preparing it for the big day when they would move in after their wedding and honeymoon. Like many young folk, they roped in the family to help with the wallpapering and painting. They had a happy future to look forward to.

The dark cloud that was to burst over the lives of Kevin and Emma formed at the beginning of February, some three months before the wedding. It was Friday the seventh and weekends were always busy for Kevin's dad who played guitar in a local band. Early that evening, he was setting up for a gig in a local club where the band had been booked to entertain the punters that night. Kevin and his mum took the opportunity to pop up to the new house to do some decorating work and Emma was down south in Glasgow for a fitting of her wedding dress. Kevin returned from the new house around 10 p.m. He had a quick shower and he was barely dry when his friend Mark Foubister called to pick Kevin up for a game of pool at Carters' Bar in the town.

The first signs of concern emerged on the Saturday morning when there was no sign of Kevin looking for his breakfast and then it was found that his bed had clearly not been slept in that night. Hugh and June were anxious – this was not normal – and they tried to contact Mark by phone but without success. They then decided to get the car out and go looking for Kevin. By sheer luck, they soon came on Mark sitting in his car parked at the roadside and they drew alongside.

A remarkable exchange followed. When Mark was told that Kevin had not come home the previous night, he roared out, 'Oh no!' and put his head in his hands, obviously seriously concerned. This alarmed Kevin's parents so much that they were now convinced something had happened to their son – so convinced that they called at the local police office and reported Kevin missing. The sergeant on duty explained the normal procedure, saying that twenty-four hours would have to pass before Kevin could officially become a missing person.

So the family took the only course open to them and recruited friends and relatives to help in the search for their son. One of the helpers was Kevin's uncle Allan McLeod from nearby Alness. In the coming years, he was to play a pivotal role in the family's fight to convince the legal authorities that Kevin had died as a result of foul play.

During the daylight hours of the Saturday, searches of the harbour and waterfront were done and a relative in the coastguard service was of particular help in this. But the hunt for Kevin McLeod continued even after darkness had fallen and right through the night till dawn. When Kevin had been missing for the required twenty-four hours, the police told the family that they were seeking the services of a diver to search the harbour. And, shortly before noon on the Sunday, when two officers called at the McLeod home, they really didn't need to speak – it was obvious they were the bearers of bad news. The officers said a body fitting the description of Kevin had been found in the harbour on the bottom under twenty feet of water. They went on to say there were no suspicious circumstances – an amazing claim since the body was, at that stage, still lying on the seabed. The parents identified their son at a local mortuary after it had been recovered from the harbour.

At this point, the family had been told that an investigation, which included interviewing the town's taxi drivers who were on duty at the material times, was taking place. Whether this was a deliberate lie or just a case of one hand not knowing what the other hand was doing is unclear but it turned out that no such investigating or interviewing had been done as it seemed as if the police had already decided that Kevin had died as a result of a tragic accident.

From my time as a detective on the streets of Glasgow, I know that a city murder squad has it knocked into them that the first twenty-four hours of any suspicious death investigation are of paramount importance. When I was a serving officer, we would treat a death as possible murder at least until after the post-mortem. So, at the time the police informed the McLeods that 'there were no suspicious circumstances', they could not possibly be sure of this – for all they knew, he could have been stabbed or shot. But their initial diagnosis would determine the path that the inquiry would follow – in this case, 'accidental death'.

My investigations turned up an intriguing fact – Kevin had apparently left home for Carters' Bar but, at one point, he had been in the Waterfront nightclub and, during an altercation there, he had been punched. The police had been told this but took no action. Over the course of the evening, Kevin had left Mark to go to a hole in the wall for some money. Mark had followed him a short time later but somehow he had missed him. Mark then started to look for Kevin. There were two roads that could have been taken and it turned out that Mark chose to take the wrong one and the friends became separated.

Kevin's death was officially recorded as drowning and 'an abdominal injury' and he was laid to rest on 15 February 1997. At that time, the family wrongly believed that the police were investigating the death as possible murder. Although this was not the case, the police did tell the family more details of what had happened on that tragic night – a night watchman in the harbour area had seen Kevin curled in a foetal position, casually dressed and wearing only a T-shirt in the bitter cold. Another witness confirmed this sighting. If Kevin wasn't drunk, why was he hunched up for possibly an hour, making no attempt to go home? I would guess an abdominal injury could be the cause.

The post-mortem showed that Kevin had a ruptured spleen and, in my long career, I have seen many such injuries caused by a violent kick. Indeed, I have attended post-mortems where the pathologist has remarked, 'Oh, we have a ruptured spleen – looks like you have a murder on your hands.'

So why was there such reluctance by the police in this case to treat the death as a murder? The public never gives much thought to the internal politics in a police force but I do. This is what worries me. In the year of Kevin's death, there was another suspicious death in the region and, on this occasion, a man who had murdered his wife gave himself up to the police. That man's confession meant the police had a 100 per cent record for clearing murder cases but, if there had been two murders and only one is solved, their clearance rate drops to 50 per cent.

Of course, there are two sides to every tale and the police take on the ruptured spleen was that it had happened when Kevin collided with a bollard located near the spot where the night watchman had seen him hunkered down. The report on the original post-mortem, carried out by Scottish pathologists, included the opinion that the major abdominal injury was consistent with falling on an object similar to the bollards on Wick harbour.

The Northern Constabulary consulted a pathologist in the south. This was one of the leading forensic pathologists in the UK, Nathaniel Cary, a man who made headlines for carrying out the autopsies on Holly Wells and Jessica Chapman murdered in Soham by Ian Huntley. Among the observations in his lengthy report was that 'the finding of the fly buttons undone when the body was recovered from the water is in keeping with him urinating at the time he entered the water'. He also offered an opinion that all the factors were:

in keeping with the deceased standing on the edge of the harbour wall close to the bow of the fishing boat *Aurora* and, as the result of some free flight, to give rise to the severe and unusual nature of the abdominal injuries.

In May of the year of their son's death Kevin's parents and their lawyer attended a meeting in the procurator fiscal's office and had the findings of the post-mortem read to them. Mrs McLeod asked about the injuries to Kevin. If there was no bollard, what else could have caused her son's injuries? She was told, 'Oh, well, it could have been a kicking.'

The McLeods were far from happy about the whole business and consulted one of Glasgow's top lawyers, Cameron Fyfe. In July, they were informed that the procurator fiscal had instructed the police to conduct a new inquiry. After this, they received what, at the time, looked like a good piece of news – there would be a new Fatal Accident Inquiry. It started in May of 1998 and continued on and off till August. But the twists and turns of an unsatisfactory case were far from over. It was proposed that one potential medical witness should be excused giving evidence to the sheriff but, when Hugh McLeod objected to this, it was agreed that the witness should indeed be called but the McLeods would have to pay the witness's costs of £300. A medical expert from Glasgow's Yorkhill hospital gave evidence and she said that Kevin had two separate injuries. She discounted the bollard theory and said she could not rule out assault.

They say the devil is in the detail and I find one detail of this inquiry surprising – a constable, who was one of the last people to see Kevin alive, took the stand at 3.53 p.m. and the sheriff was told that he had to be at the airport half an hour or so later. The officer spoke only briefly before being allowed to leave catch his flight. Eventually the sheriff's determination was that the cause of injuries had not been established but that assault could not be ruled out. The anguish of the McLeods continued.

A huge blow came in October 2002 when it was announced that investigations into the death were being 'stood down' and the officers involved were returning to their normal duties. The family was devastated and, with nowhere to turn, they approached me through the organisation A Search for Justice, which now no longer exists.

I told the Crown Office of my intention to travel up to Wick. In spring 2003, I met the family and was struck by their determination to get justice for their son. Not much misses the locals in such places and the reception staff of the hotel where I was staying knew why I was there even before I picked up the room key. In the way a detective often does, I casually asked a member of staff what had happened and was told that it was common knowledge that Kevin had been given a kicking and thrown in the harbour.

At the harbour itself, I had a good look round with Hugh and June and the uncle, Allan McLeod, who impressed me with his determination to find out what really happened. Chatting to them, it was clear that, if Kevin had simply fallen in the water, the family would have accepted fate and got on with their lives. Instead, they were consumed by a feeling of injustice. Incidentally, while I was at the harbour, I was being watched carefully by a young guy. Some folk told me that, at one stage, he had been a suspect. I was careful not to go too near the edge!

I managed to speak to the night watchman who had seen Kevin hunched up and, with the harbour master's permission, he showed me where he had seen Kevin. Two other witnesses were traced and confirmed what had happened.

I wanted to speak to the skippers of the two boats that were tied up near to where Kevin was found on that tragic night. I was in luck. Detectives foraging around are not too common in Wick and the local newspaper had noted my interest. The skippers sought me out to see if they could help. All sorts of other inconsistencies turned up. The two boats were the *Aurora* and *Gunnhilda* and they had been tied up facing each other about thirty feet apart. Kevin's body had been found almost halfway between them. The skippers were of the opinion that Kevin had not struck either boat on the way down. Interestingly, they said tide was in that night. That meant that somebody could simply have stepped on to the *Gunnhilda* and, if a person had fallen on the *Aurora* at that time, the distance would have been only three or four feet. The police never interviewed the crews of the boats.

My inquiries turned up the fact that, when pathologist Dr Cary had been shown the harbour, the tide was out, meaning that the drop from the pier to the fishing boats was much greater than on the night Kevin died. I spoke to him about it and he said he had based some of his findings on the belief that Kevin would have fallen at least fifteen feet and he was annoyed that he had not been told of the state of the tide that night. He also suggested that Kevin could have hit the *Aurora* on the way down but the boat's skipper disagreed.

I continued to forage around and came across a woman who told me she had seen Kevin being attacked by three men in the harbour area but she didn't know who they were. After I told her to pull the other one, she named a man she said had done the actual kicking. From her description she gave, I realised it could have been the guy who had eyed me up on the quay earlier. This woman had been charged with giving false information to the police with regard to the attack. When I talked to the Crown Office about her, I was told she had 'done a runner'. I managed to find her but she decided against any further involvement.

Another local woman I found said that, on the day after Kevin's disappearance, her boyfriend, a well-known troublemaker, had told her that he had done something he would 'regret for the rest of [his] life' when in the company of another mystery man. When I passed this info on to the authorities, I was told that this possible suspect had declined to be interviewed. You couldn't make it up!

Despite all the effort over the years, we are no nearer obtaining justice for Kevin McLeod. It sickens me but does not surprise me. Country forces have a bad record of refusing help from big-city murder squads, preferring to do their own thing. Indeed, I have personal experience of a case when an offer of help from the Glasgow police was made. The answer from the then big-wigs in the

Northern Constabulary was, 'We can solve our own murders – we don't need help from outside forces.'

There is currently much debate about restructuring police resources – not before time. Cases like those of Innes Ewart and Kevin McLeod show the need for it. I believe two families could have been spared much anguish if the real murder squad experts, the men and woman who hunt killers on a day-to-day basis, had been called in. If only . . .

2

PIRATES OF THE LONDON ROAD

A weekend trip to the 'Barras' is a Glasgow tradition. I doubt if there is a family in the city that hasn't made a pilgrimage to the noisy, untidy, crowded stalls, off London Road, in search of a bargain. Even if you don't buy anything, there is free entertainment aplenty. As street markets go, it is world famous and deservedly so – all your shopping needs can be satisfied in a place that is so far removed from the atmosphere of a modern chromium and concrete US-style mall that it seems to have come from another planet. Maybe that is putting it a bit too strongly but the Barras are certainly a throwback to another time and another way of life – one-stop shopping that is gallus rather than glitzy.

As a young cop, I spent plenty of time in there, little realising that, when I retired from the force, it would still be a place where I would continue to exercise my detective skills. Every cop on the beat knows his way round the Barras. On a Sunday, there can be thousands of visitors, some from overseas who might not be to up to speed on the habits Glasgow's get-rich-quick merchants, and often there are only three of four cops to control the crowds and try to clamp down on the scams that tempt the lowlife who mingle with the majority of honest registered merchants.

Incidentally, there was a police connection with the Barras since day one for the legendary Maggie McIver, the founder and driving force of the place, was the daughter of an Ayrshire copper. Maggie became a real Glasgow character. Her career as an entrepreneur started on a street in Parkhead when, aged just twelve, she looked after a fruit barrow belonging to a friend of her mother. A born trader, Maggie thrived in the cut and thrust of selling from street barrows, a business where a cheery personality and ready wit with the punters were as important as fresh produce. Maggie soon saved up enough to open a small fruit and veg place in Bridgeton. Running it meant frequent early-morning trips to the fruit market and, on one of her regular visits, she met James McIver who she later married.

They went into business together renting horses and carts to traders who hawked around the wealthier areas of the west end. It was all going well for the McIvers and they bought some ground in Moncur Street in the east end where they rented static barrows to street traders to hawk their wares on Saturday mornings. And so the Barras were born. The original site is still in use though the area has obviously expanded greatly. This was shortly after the turn of the twentieth century and the Barras was to grow and prosper for more than a hundred years.

The Barrowland Ballroom was built above the stalls and it attracted dancing-daft Glasgow folk in huge numbers. It survives to this day, often hosting the biggest names in rock and pop. The ballroom also made headlines in the late sixties as the place where a so-called serial killer, who was nicknamed Bible John, picked up his victims. There is now much doubt about whether or not the three dancehall killings attributed to Bible John were, in fact, the work of one man. However, all that is pretty much ancient history – the Barras thrive today though much has changed since old Maggie first hawked fruit from a barrow.

In the early days, street people of all kinds threw a hat on the pavement and tried to convince the throngs of bargain hunters to toss a few pence into it as a reward for their skills at singing, scratching a tune out of a fiddle, juggling or whatever. For a spell 'strong man' acts and even escapologists, in the Houdini mould, would draw a crowd. These days are over now and the entertainment is of a different kind.

The majority of traders at the Barras are honest folk trying to turn of bob or two selling legitimate goods, albeit at prices below those in shops. But, Glasgow being Glasgow, there are always a few ready to try to take on the law. One Australian visitor told me of the regular laughs he had watching the sellers of illegal tobacco in the streets. They carry no satchels – the pouches of 'snout' are secreted into the pockets of their trousers or jacket if they are wearing one. If there are no cops in sight they move around the crowds shouting their wares at the top of their voices but, the minute they sniff a cop in the air, they go quiet and melt into the crowd looking for all the world like an ordinary Joe hunting a bargain. When the boys in blue move on, out comes the tobacco and the unlicensed vendors are back in noisy action.

All this may have amused my Australian friend but more than suspect baccy is sold at the Barras. Much more serious stuff also goes on with unscrupulous dealers doing a brisk trade in pirated DVDs, computer software and the like and that's where I came back on the scene. After my official police career ended in the early eighties, you could say I went into the entertainment business myself. I had been a copper on the beat and murder squad detective for twenty-six years and, to my own astonishment, my new career would last seventeen years. The offer of a new job come 'out of the blue' which was apt for someone who had spent so many years 'in the blue'! An old contact in the London police had been asked to form an organisation called the Federation Against Copyright Theft (FACT) to represent film companies and others who were beginning to be ripped off through the sale of pirate videos and all sorts of other breaches of copyright. He needed a man in Scotland and I got the job. Amusingly he told me during the interview that two million illegal copies of the video of *ET* had been sold. Always keen to get the facts right, I told him, 'Make that two million and one!' We got on well after that.

The video pirates and others involved in copyright theft were making fortunes and getting a pretty free run at it from the police in various big cities and the trading standards officers who were too overworked or simply 'not bovvered' to paraphrase that talented TV comedy actress Catherine Tate's catchphrase. But it has to be said it is a difficult area for the investigator trained in day-to-day police work. I had a lot to learn and went south to London for some serious instruction in the ways of the entertainment business. The office, a pretty palatial place compared with police stations in the rough areas of Glasgow, was near Oxford Circus. It might have been an impressive address for the notepaper but it was a nightmare for an employee to get to. I used to park the car miles away and hoof it to the centre of the great metropolis. My colleagues and I were given an introduction to the workings of the film industry – film sales methods, production details, the intricacies of video production and the various hi- and low-tech ways of making fakes. It was intriguing stuff.

The counterfeit films were mostly sold at car boot sales and markets. With thousands of bargain hunters in one place, many of them not in the least worried that they were buying pirated goods provided the price was right, Barrowland was ideal for the pirates.

At first, FACT gave me Scotland and Newcastle to cover. They supplied a company car and told me to get on with protecting the interests of their members which included most of the major film-making companies and the BBC. Apart from the Barras, my patch included the huge Ingliston Market adjacent to Edinburgh International Airport. I may say that, right from the start, I got assistance, whenever possible, from the Glasgow Trading Standards folk though the same could not be said of their Edinburgh counterparts. We had some early successes and some fun. My old contacts in the underworld and my knowledge of the way the Glasgow neds work helped me curb some the excesses at the Barras where you could buy DVDs of recently released Hollywood films for a fiver. Well, some were recently released but some were even newer than that as this tale of a Glaswegian picked up at the airport will show.

A well-known shoplifter, let's call him John Kerr, had just flown in to Glasgow from the States with hundreds of silk scarves in his possession. There was nothing new in that but he also had a videocassette that had a label reading *Men in Black* on the spine. This started the customs guys talking about what to do with the film. Kerr interrupted them to say he knew an ex-cop, a guy called Les Brown, who worked for the film companies. He knocked them out with the remark that I had arrested him on a murder charge many years ago!

I got the call but, before heading on to the M8 to the airport, I phoned FACT's head office to ask about *Men in Black* and was told no one had heard of it.

Before customs officers and I got down to the pirate film stuff, they wanted the full story of the murder charge so I gave it to them. The first time I met Kerr, I was told that he was a highly skilled shoplifter – the best in the city, perhaps the best in the country. He was based in a pub on the banks of the Clyde and such was his fame that he shoplifted to order, getting the actual goods his customers wanted rather than stealing any old rubbish and then trying to find a sucker to buy it. He dealt in the best of stuff.

An example of his style was the time he was approached in the pub by a guy who wanted a really expensive suit on the cheap. John eyed the guy up in a manner reminiscent of a hangman calculating a villain's drop or an undertaker sizing you for a coffin. He told the punter to come back in an hour and, when he duly returned, he was offered three perfectly fitting Daks suits at £100 each or £250 the lot. The gear had been stolen from Frasers in Buchanan Street. Although John Kerr was known to the store's staff, he still had the ability to nick stuff without being spotted. Incidentally, he told the customs guys that he hoped some of the silk scarves would be sold to the sales assistants in Frasers! That was the guy I arrested for murder.

I had received a call to assist a beat constable in trouble at a house in the Gorbals (at the time I was in the serious crime squad). There had been a fight between a notorious cowboy builder called Gallagher (who specialised in defrauding old folk with fake roof repairs) and another man. The two had apparently been fighting over the 'lady' who owned the house. In the course of the scuffle, the cowboy had been bottled and staggered from the flat gushing blood. He was found dead nearby. Just before the body was discovered the other man had, for some reason, mentioned my name to the cop. He had fled by the time I arrived, but the constable's description made me convinced the suspect was Kerr. We checked a lot of his known haunts before finding him, sleeping like a baby without a care in the world, in a bed in a flat in Castlemilk. It seemed a shame to wake him but I tweaked his big toe and, before he knew much about what was going on, he was locked up in Craigie Street nick, just off Victoria Road, charged with murder.

There was laughter in court a few months later when Kerr was in the dock in the High Court, explaining that he was awakened and arrested by 'Big Les'. This prompted the judge to ask, 'Who is Big Les?' 'Him,' said Kerr, pointing across the court to where I was sitting. The charge was reduced to culpable homicide and he got eight years. 'Just what Big Les said would happen,' said Kerr. More laughter. The judge's face was, as they say, a picture.

With all that history out of the way, back at the airport, we turned our attention to the pirate video. We released Kerr and I went into action to try to find out about the film. It was a top-class comedy starring Will Smith and Tommy Lee Jones though, to me, some of the supporting cast looked like they really had been dropped in from outer space. At this stage, the film had not even been released for showing in cinemas. We called Hollywood and found that the film was still in production and the first cuts were only available to the editor and some of his staff. I was asked the serial number at the start of the film that Kerr had and Hollywood confirmed that the number referred to *Men in Black* which was still in the editing suite!

The next call was from the FBI, asking me to find out from Kerr how the hell he had got hold of such a film.

He told me:

At the far end of Broadway, at the foot of the Twin Towers, there are several short streets that lead down to the river. One is a dead end. As you enter this street, there's an expensive shoe shop and next to that a Chinese shop. That's where I bought the film for ten dollars.

The feds and a posse of New York's finest, in their uniforms, raided the place and picked up 500 pirate videos. It turned out that the man behind the bootlegging operation worked in the Hollywood studio's editing suite. It was a satisfactory conclusion but I couldn't help wondering about the greed of folk who would steal films that had not even been released and reviewed and sell them for peanuts. Kerr was pretty pleased with himself and asked what his reward for his role would be. 'You don't go to jail,' I told him.

We held frequent meetings on video bootlegging. Some were good copies but the quality of others was dreadful – sometimes the videos were produced from a film taken by a crook sitting in a cinema with a camera. Hollywood execs used to fly across the pond, no doubt at huge expense, to talk to us about the problem. They didn't have much of a sense of humour or realism and, on one occasion, when I pointed out that the problem would go away if they made their videos cheap enough to challenge the pirates, I was met with a deafening silence. Cutting the profit was clearly not a route that appealed to them.

It was a curious business and one of the big problems was not nabbing the sellers but finding who was making the copies. Once we raided a place in Coatbridge where sixty recorders were action at one time, all churning out the bootleg stuff. It was also difficult to get cases to court. Procurator fiscals consider problems in rough areas to be more pressing than pursuing the odd pirate video and protecting the profits of wealthy film companies. In my seventeen years with FACT, not one video pirate was sent to jail.

However, that didn't stop us trying to nail them at every opportunity. I remember being asked to assist on a visit to video shop in London's notorious East End. The guys in the south had not bothered to tell me that the place was owned and run by a local gangster hard man who had earlier refused FACT access to the shop unless they had a search warrant, which they didn't have. This time, three of us went in to the shop where we were confronted by the owner whose face was criss-crossed by Mars bars as the Glasgow cops call scars. I asked this fearsome character if there was any chance of a cuppa. He replied that we could have tea but it would take a minute or two as the kettle was on the blink. I said that was OK and we would take a wee look at the back shop while he was seeing to the tea. Through the back, we found VCRs hammering out copy after copy of pirated films. Life on the hard streets of Glasgow helps you develop the kind of brass neck you don't get in more genteel parts. On another occasion in London, I remember an Asian shop owner naively asking if we were going to look into the basement. 'We are now!' I replied. More VCRs were churning away and this time it was copies of Asian films that we found.

Back at the Barras we had identified an easy-going young guy (let's call him Ian) who was coining it in and I despaired of getting the police interested – in their view, they had bigger fish to fry – but I got a break. A new officer, Pat Ferguson, had arrived at London Road Station, the cop shop nearest to the Barras. Pat and I were on the same wavelength. He wanted action. I was called to a Sunday-morning meet. More than a hundred cops were there plus plain-clothes officers who had been doing undercover work identifying targets. On a signal, we descended en masse, even blocking off streets round the market. Forty illegal stallholders were arrested and the seized goods piled high in the police gym where the

TV reporters and the newspaper crime guys assembled to look at the haul. I was asked on camera how much the goods were worth. I immediately said ten million pounds. When the fuss was over I was asked by the divisional commander of the raid how I had arrived at that figure. With a straight face, I told him it was easy for an expert like me. Happy days.

The travelling to and from Newcastle, which was originally in my patch, was becoming wearing and I was delighted when Richard Armstrong was taken on as a FACT investigator based there. He was a tiptop acquisition and we worked well together. On one occasion, in the Johnstone area, we intercepted and charged the drivers of fourteen ice-cream vans with possession of pirate videos. They were fined £400 each.

When videos pass from hand to hand or are given to charities, sometimes it is not all that easy for folk not in the business to know what is genuine and what is not. FACT's head office asked me to look in on the world-famous Rachel House Children's Hospice at Kinross in Fife, a place where very ill young children are looked after with love, care and understanding. We had no real problems and any slight concerns were amicably dealt with. After promising to help in any way I could, I left the hospice.

I was soon put to the test in my new role as gofer for Rachel House. Two of the youngsters, both very seriously ill, were great fans of Glasgow Rangers and had said they would love a visit from a player. An ex-cop I knew was then head of security at Ibrox, Rangers' stadium. We knew we had to work fast and a visit was quickly arranged to take place in a couple of days' time at 3 p.m. I phoned the hospice with the good news and Mrs Notman, then in charge, asked which player would be coming. I said I didn't know but that someone from the club would definitely be there. At the appointed hour, the two young lads were in the car park wearing their replica Rangers football strips when a Parks of Hamilton coach pulled up and out stepped the entire team. Some household names were in tears on the way home.

The Hollywood connections also helped me help CHAS (the Children's Hospice Association Scotland). They asked me to run a raffle and I needed prizes. I knew the folk at Disney and asked for a holiday for four people. 'Paris?' they asked. 'Florida,' I said. And they gave me it. American Airlines chipped in with flights and, with the assistance of Maq Rasul of Global Video, we sold 30,000 tickets at a quid each – neat little raffle! Still on the show business tack, Sharleen Spiteri, the lead singer with Texas, came to the hospice's Glasgow office and was snapped during a photo shoot putting a smart new nameplate on its door. She and the band became big supporters of CHAS, as did Ewan McGregor.

Soon I found myself having to do some FACT negotiating with Stagecoach and I met the company's millionaire owners, Brian Soutar and Anne Gloag. Always at the cutting edge in the transport business, they had decided to entertain their bus passengers with videos and I had to advise them on the situation with regard to licences. I always enjoy a bit of a wind-up and had some fun with this nice couple, both of whom offer great support to various charities. I always referred to their vehicles in the good old Glasgow terms as buses. The luxury coaches – complete with video equipment – were, in their owners' eyes, something rather more special than buses. They didn't talk about buses. Whenever we meet now, we have a laugh about that day and 'life on the coaches' as we should perhaps say.

Back in London, the film moguls were sick of piracy and, whenever a new blockbuster came out, they were always trying to think of new ways to outfox the perpetrators. However, they didn't take into account the ways of your average Scottish lorry driver.

When the movie *The Return of the Jedi* was due out, the same system was to be followed worldwide on its release. The movement of the copies of the film to the cinemas showing it had to be tracked by organisations like FACT. We had to track one copy from a depot in Glasgow to Aviemore. A national security firm was used to transport it. When I asked the company if it had gone directly from Glasgow to its Highland destination, I was told it had not – it went by way of Edinburgh. I then asked if it went directly from the capital to Aviemore. Apparently not – after Edinburgh, it went to Dundee and, from there, the firm took it to Aberdeen, Inverness and on to Aviemore, the famous outdoors resort.

We then had to check all was OK on the film's circuitous journey north so I interviewed the driver of the van that had transported the huge metal containers holding the blockbuster. He said it had been dropped at the cinema and, when I asked him if he had a receipt for delivery, he surprised me by saying he didn't. He had arrived at the cinema at 8 a.m. and naturally nobody had been about at that time so the valuable film had been left at the cinema's front door. My report to Hollywood on how we handled valuable films confirmed that, if the pirates in London had tried hard enough, they could have picked up a copy of this film from a Highland doorstep – plus half a dozen rolls and a pint of milk!

I was beginning to feel I had enough of the Pirates of Britain, never mind the Caribbean, but there was to be another interesting episode before I finally gave up as a guardian of copyright. In 1995, the blockbuster to catch the headlines was *Braveheart* starring Mel Gibson. In the comfort of my south-side home, I watched the TV coverage of all the stars arriving for the premiere and, as Gibson wandered around in full Highland gear, I began to take more than a passing interest – in fact, I nearly spilled my cuppa – when I saw some people in the crowd start passing around leaflets to anyone who would take them. The flyers featured Mel Gibson in his role as William Wallace, complete with the trademark face paint associated with the film. The idea of the leaflet was to cash in on the pro-Scottish sentiments of the film and encourage people to join the Scottish National Party. It seemed to me a blatant breach of the Copyright, Designs and Patents Act 1988. It was enough to get me to jump into the FACT-mobile early next day and head for the capital and the headquarters of the party.

The usual frosty receptionist asked my business and I said I wanted to speak to the person in charge. The usual interrogation followed – do you have an appointment and what is your business? With a bit of a frosty face myself, I declared that I was attempting to stop the SNP going into liquidation. That did the trick and, moments later, I was speaking to one of the top bananas in the party, Mike Russell. I told him about the breach of copyright in using the still from the film for political purposes and that only a recovery of the leaflets – virtually impossible – would appease the film-makers. He took a minute or two to realise I was serious.

After I got home, I received an interesting call. On Gibson's return to the States, the Hollywood moguls apparently asked him how the trip to Scotland had gone. He told them about the leaflets being handed out and asked if it was OK for the political party to have done that. The answer was, of course, that it was not and Hollywood got in touch with FACT in London. FACT were able to tell the States that their Scottish investigator was already on the case. It was all resolved amicably since the use of the *Braveheart* picture had been an unintentional breach of copyright and it was resolved on a personal basis between the top people on both organisations with an apology given and accepted.

There was another Mel Gibson/*Braveheart* incident in my time with FACT. The film was released in September 1995 around the time the Scottish football team was due to play a friendly at Hampden and the team was staying at Troon before the game. A friend who does video work for the Scottish Football Association said that the players would like to watch *Braveheart* on video at the hotel. At that time, it was not available in video stores in the UK. But, like a good Scottish fan, I took it upon myself to make sure the 'boys' got what they wanted.

I got in touch with the States and a copy of the film, converted to the PAL format from the US NTSC format, was sent to me. It was all done under conditions of strictest security. As FACT's man, I insisted the video never left my sight so, down in Troon, I enjoyed a nice dinner with the players before we all settled down to watch Gibson playing William Wallace. The lads loved it but the final scenes of Wallace being tortured got them a bit worked up in anger. One star, already known as a bit of a tough guy on the field, turned to me and remarked that it was a pity they weren't playing England the next day.

In recent years, our results against the old enemy have not been too great. Maybe I should ask Walter Smith to make showing *Braveheart* before games against the white shirts a ritual!

3

LIFE AND DEATH ON THE STREETS

A long career as an investigator, official and private, is guaranteed to make you develop a deep hatred of the drug trade. Time after time, you see at first-hand what addiction can do to people and the lengths it drives them to in order to feed their habits.

Much petty crime in cities is fuelled by the kind of lowlife who would rob a blind man's begging bowl to pay for a few grams. All that is bad enough but it is sickening to see what drugs can do to beautiful young women. Prostitutes are often drug users and their addictions force them into a very dangerous way of life on the streets. Some pay with their lives as well as their looks.

Cops on the beat will mix with prostitutes right from the very start of their careers. The girls are out on the streets after dark and they deal with all sorts of strange punters and see a lot going on. Most of them have good relationships with the cops and will be ready to provide helpful information when they can. They are aware that, as well as having the ability to huckle them, the cops can also sometimes be in the position to save their lives.

Those who manage to survive in this nasty business can be shrewd cookies indeed.

A woman I will call Sadie is a good example. I remember getting a distress call from her one night. Her husband, no doubt fed up with her and her way of life, had thrown her out on to Allison Street in the south side of Glasgow, a patch I know well. Her sister lived in nearby Govanhill but she was away and would not return till the next day. Sadie had been of assistance to me in an investigation and now turned to me for help. I got in the car and headed to Allison Street and soon found her wandering about. By this time, it was the wee sma' hours and she was some sight as she got into the car (I hoped no one I knew was watching!). She was in full glam working gear, short skirt, shiny black boots, dripping with cheap jewellery etc. but the heavy mascara was running down both cheeks and tears were not far away.

I took her to a local hotel and told the night porter who I was and said that Sadie was a vital witness we were protecting from gangsters by moving her around hotels. The guy was goggle-eyed at the appearance of Sadie, not normally the sort of girl who pitched up in his hotel. I paid in advance and left satisfied that I had done the right thing. The next day I got a call from Sadie who said she was now off to stay with her sister and could I meet her so that she could repay me for the bed and breakfast. When she handed a few notes over, I asked her where she had got the cash – when I had picked her up she was stony broke. She smiled and told me that the hotel I had taken her to was much used by commercial travellers and the like and that she had 'made a few quid' during the night! Such is a life in prostitution.

Mostly, cops' dealings with street girls are much less amusing. The oldest profession is also perhaps the most dangerous and, for a detective, solving the murder of a prostitute is often challenging. Obviously, for a start, the usual appeals for anyone with information to come forward often fall on deaf ears. The sleaze merchants who kerb-crawl don't see it as a duty to let the world know what they get up to after dark even if it could help solve a murder. But, as anyone who follows the tabloids knows, girls are killed by their clients – sadly on an all-too-regular basis. But I can assure you that the police put as much effort into solving these hard cases as they do for any murder.

I was involved in one such high-profile case and it was a frustrating experience. A lot of old-fashioned detective work went into it but without success. This was the infamous murder of Jacqueline Gallagher. Jacqueline was a good-looker and it was hard to believe that she had turned to the streets. Drugs were to blame. The amount of cash needed to feed a habit is remarkable and, for many girls, prostitution is a quick fix – an easy way to fill the syringe and avoid the agony of life without drugs.

Jacqueline's death had been making headlines on and off for years before her mother turned to A Search for Justice in July 2005. Her daughter was twenty-six when she was found dead in a lay-by in Bowling not far from the north end of the Erskine Bridge in June 1996. There was massive media coverage of the discovery of her body which had been found in bushes wrapped in a curtain. After some initial difficulty, the body was identified. And not long after came a surprise move. As I have pointed out, it is not normal for prostitutes' clients to identify themselves but, in this case, one did and, indeed, he did more than just admit to being a client. A man called George Johnstone, from Erskine, visited the murder incident room claiming to be have been one of Jacqueline's clients and, most significantly, offering to give a DNA sample. Amazingly, this offer was declined and that decision was to have remarkable consequences years later.

The murder of Jacqueline Gallagher remains unsolved. But it is interesting to look at what happened to the investigation at the time and later. CCTV is of great assistance to the detective and, in this case, hours were spent poring over footage from Glasgow's red light area, the streets around Blythswood Square. Suspect vehicles were noted and investigated. It was time-consuming routine work but that is often the road to success in a murder investigation.

After all the initial flurry of activity, the trail went cold but later George Johnstone was making newspaper headlines. He was involved in a fatal road accident in Paisley, stood trial and was found guilty. His DNA was taken and it matched DNA connected with Jacqueline's murder. He had, of course, originally offered his DNA and, without any coercion, he claimed to have been a client.

After his release from prison on the motoring charges, he was arrested and charged with killing Jacqueline. He went to trial and was freed on a not proven verdict. Clearly, among other things, the jury were unhappy with the fact that his offer to DNA at the time had not even been taken up by the police. This was the situation when I came on board at the invitation of Jacqueline's mother.

Johnstone offered to let me interview him but I decided not to, preferring to approach this complicated puzzle in my own way. I went to Dumbarton Police Station where I met Detective Superintendent Ken Watters, a man with a caseload of unsolved murders he had been delegated to investigate. The Gallagher case was not one of them. Ken was approachable and helpful. In the initial investigation, there had been some concern about a red Citroën van. Despite Ken not being involved in the case, when he knew I was coming, he read through the papers. He told me that more than 700 such vans had been investigated and that intensive inquiries had been made on 'action forms'. An action form is made out with the registration number and the name of the owner of all the vehicles that could possibly have been at a crime scene. The forms are sent to the area where the vehicle is based and the local police then try to find out from the owner where the vehicle was at the significant time. If possible, an officer will also take a look at the vehicle. The forms are then sent back to the originating office.

I thought taking a look at the forms that had been completed in the Jacqueline Gallagher case might be helpful but, to do so, I needed to apply for permission under the Freedom of Information Act. No joy – I never got to see the forms. It seems Strathclyde Police did not want me to investigate this murder but I pressed on. With the help of Jacqueline's mother and newspaper cuttings, I found two witnesses who claimed to have seen the suspect vehicle around the place where the body had been found at the material time.

One was a man I will call Robert. He lived in Old Kilpatrick, in the shadow of the Erskine Bridge, and a short distance from Bowling. He told me that he was out walking his dog at 6 a.m. and, as he approached the lay-by, he saw a red Citroën van. The back of the van was facing him and the rear doors were open. He said that it was empty apart from dustsheets. He became aware of noises in nearby bushes and saw a man struggling with what appeared to be a heavy carpet. He said he knew a bit about vans and that he was certain the vehicle was a Citroën. He said there was lettering on the van and remembered seeing the words 'Causeyside' and 'free estimates'. In my view, this was an honest and reliable witness. Another witness was a guy we can call James. He said he and two workmates saw a red Citroën van parked rather carelessly in the lay-by. He said they particularly remembered it because it was so badly parked it could have interfered with other traffic.

James and his mates also claimed to have seen something being dumped in the bushes and assumed it was a heavy carpet or something similar – sadly, people dumping at the roadside is no unusual occurrence. The three men proceeded up the A82 towards Loch Lomond and stopped at the lights near the garage at the junction for Helensburgh. The garage is well known locally as Jackie Stewart's because it was once owned by the racing driver's family and, as they waited for the green light, the red Citroën drew alongside. When the driver noticed they were having a good look at him, he ducked down as if to hide his face. James thought the van had the word 'Design' painted on it in an artistic fashion.

The two vehicles drove off and passed through several roundabouts which would have given the van driver the chance to go in the opposite direction if he thought he was being followed. The driver, however, didn't turn back at any of these roundabouts but he did veer right towards Balloch at the bottom of the Loch Lomond road and that was the last James saw of the van again. James said he jotted the van's registration number down but he lost a bit of paper he had written it on.

When the police were told all this, they were unimpressed and said the witnesses were unreliable because they had talked of seeing the van on two different days. The police also said the two witnesses' descriptions of how the van was parked did not tally. The police were dismissive about the heavy carpet, pointing out that it was a light curtain that had been found with the body.

I went back to James and Robert and they both told me the same story about how the van had been parked. And they said the sightings were on the same day. I was sure they had seen the body being disposed of and that the driver was possibly a painter and decorator who lived east of Balloch, an area that could include Bonhill, Jamestown and even Stirling. The media were of great assistance and descriptions of the driver and the van were widely circulated but nothing was turned up.

It occurred to me that, taking into account the frequency of attacks on prostitutes, the killer of Jacqueline could have struck before and might strike again – hence my desire to have a look at the action forms on the 700 vans. But, unfortunately, it was not to be and the mystery of who killed Jacqueline lives on.

Another tragic case in a similar mould is that of Emma Caldwell. She too had turned to prostitution to pay for drugs and was found dumped in a remote area near Biggar in May 2005. Newspapers made much of the beauty of this girl, printing pictures of her before her descent into prostitution and addiction and what she looked like at the time of her death. The contrast was hellish. She had been living in a women's hostel on the south side and CCTV cameras got horrifying pictures of her drug-ravaged face as she went to ply her trade in the city centre. I had a friend who knew her in the old days and he said she was so strikingly beautiful that she stopped conversations when she entered a room. Drugs wrecked her. No wonder we want to show drug dealers no mercy.

But girls, drugs and prostitution will continue to go together so what should we do? I believe the answer is licensed brothels, like they have in Holland – strictly run and with medical supervision. Street prostitution should be a crime that is cracked down on toughly. It might not happen and, until it does, I would have a maximum police presence in red-light areas. I would also advocate the use of CCTV cameras in these places and the punters' car registration numbers being recorded.

A number plate played a role in an interesting case involving prostitution in my days with the Serious Crime Squad. Some of the girls on the street told the cops they were a bit worried about a guy who cruised the red-light district in a sports car with what could be a personalised number plate – an indication right away that the driver might not be the sharpest tack in the box. Several of the girls said he was a weirdo and very violent.

A few nights later, a colleague and I were in the Blythswood Square area in a squad car when we saw a car that looked suspiciously like the one the girls had mentioned. The driver had a passenger, a young woman, but, since we had not seen her get in the car, we did not know whether or not she was on the game. Anyway, we stopped the car and spoke to the couple separately. Conscious that the girl could simply be an innocent acquaintance of the driver, I spoke to her very carefully. I had to point out to her that we had had reports of a weirdo in just such a car and I asked if she was happy to continue her journey. She thanked us and indicated that she didn't have a problem and the couple drove off. My colleagues confirmed the driver's identity and found he stayed in Paisley Road West not far from Ibrox, home of Glasgow Rangers.

We will call the guy John X. The night we stopped the car was a long and busy one but, nonetheless, before we logged off at 7 a.m., we drove over to Paisley Road West and had a look at the address the driver had given. Sure enough, the car was there and, at that time, we never gave a thought to the fact that perhaps we should have taken firmer action when we stopped John X in Blythswood Square.

Back at work at 11 p.m. the next night, we were shocked to hear that a prostitute had been seriously assaulted by a sports car driver. And she told the officers on the case that, soon after she had been picked up, the car had been stopped by police and one of the officers had warned her about the driver. I phoned the cop in charge of the case, told her what had happened and that we knew who the driver was. She had no objection to us paying him a visit.

When we got there, the car was parked outside and we gave the door a knock. Cruising the red-light area in an eye-catching and easily identifiable car was not the brightest of moves as I earlier observed but John X had another surprise for us. My opening words – to be repeated months later at Glasgow High Court – were 'Do you remember me?'

He replied, 'Yes, you're the policeman who spoke to me last night.' Reverse identification! In one sentence, he had identified both himself and me. Without hesitation, we took him off to the Central where John X was charged with attempted murder. As we took him away, I remember thinking it was odd that, at the time we arrested him – three o'clock in the morning – his wife, a teacher, had not been in the house.

We had impounded the sports car and, a few days later, a prostitute, who was at the office making inquiries, noticed it and told the CID that she had been assaulted by the driver of the car. She went into great detail of the horrific and perverted attack. The accused took part in identification parades and, after being picked out by other prostitutes, further charges followed.

But the tale was far from over. Our original informant, the prostitute who had told us about the car, came back to the office to say that John X's wife had been in a pub in Maryhill looking for a heavy to threaten witnesses who might testify against her husband. It so happened that she was given the name of someone who could fit the bill and that guy happened to be the husband of the woman who had told us about the number plate. A meeting was arranged and the so-called heavy was given £400. I told the informant to keep the cash and put it about that witnesses would be silenced. Then I went to the procurator fiscal who consulted with the Crown Office and they backed this rather unusual course of action I had taken.

It was amusing that on the day of the High Court trial when John X entered the dock and was seen to get a thumbs up from his wife. But there was a surprise in store for him. Silenced witnesses? What silenced witnesses? One after another, prostitutes and other witnesses identified him as the attacker. It was, as they say, a no-brainer and the jury wasted no time in finding him guilty. He got ten years – a good result.

After the case was over, I went back to the fiscal with another question – what was to happen to the £400 given to the prostitute's husband as part of the silenced witness scam? The reply I got delighted me. 'What £400?'

4

HELL IN A HOLIDAY CAMP

Rape is one of the most horrific of crimes – and one of the most difficult to deal with. I had some experience of investigating it in my time as an officer in the Strathclyde force but it was with A Search for Justice that I saw another side of this despicable crime. It was an eye-opener to me, a former detective with years of experience of life on the streets of Glasgow. All the old arguments about rape and the difficulty of proving it and the danger of false accusation are regularly rehearsed in crime books and articles. Even the law has problems with it – rape is dealt with differently under the Scottish legal system from the way it is treated in England, particularly in how the crime is reported in the media. Up here, we are rightly extremely careful about preserving the anonymity of the victim – another example, to my mind, of the superiority of Scots Law over the English version.

Anonymity is vital – rape often results in victims of the crime being mentally scarred for life and the last thing they need is the added distress of having their names appear in the media. Even the successful conviction of an offender can be of little consolation to a woman violated in this manner, something that the psychologists have been examining for years. In some respects, being a rape victim is like no other type of victim: the ramifications run deep into the subconscious for years, perhaps for a lifetime. It can not be shrugged off in the way some other crimes are ultimately forgotten, buried under the pressure of getting on with life. For the victim and the family concerned, the anguish is horrific. And sometimes, as in the tale I am about to tell, that anguish is added to by, of all people, the police.

Ninety-nine per cent of folk who have had a holiday in a holiday camp take home happy memories. Many return to such places as Butlins in Ayr year after year. For some people, a fortnight in the company of the Redcoats, the excitement of bingo, ballroom dancing, variety shows, cheery modern bars and friendly company are a lure they can't resist. Each week during the cold dark winter months, they carefully put away some cash, hoarding it to pay for a sunshine break that they look forward to all year.

And it has to be said that, among the younger clientele of such places, up and down the land, the somewhat mysterious and exciting thing that's called 'chalet life' is also an attraction. Teenagers by the thousands have had their first real experience of what is coyly called the opposite sex in such camps. Generally, it is all pretty harmless fun, the stuff of growing up and experiencing the ways of the world but this was not the case for two girls I will call Linda and Susan who came to my attention in a Search for Justice investigation.

Holiday camps also attract young folk looking for seasonal work. The thought of a pleasant month or two earning a bit of cash in the company of like-minded folk appealed to Linda, a tall, leggy and attractive nineteen-year-old. She worked as a waitress in Butlins at Ayr in 1998 and, instead of spending a carefree summer, she found herself at the centre of a nightmare.

The horror story began in the early hours of the 23 May. She was making her way back to her chalet after work and a bit of a night out when another employee, a security guard she vaguely knew by sight, offered to accompany her home. This he did but, when Linda went to close the door of the chalet behind her, she realised he had managed to slip into the room. She was thrown to the floor and raped. She reported the attack to the head of security and insisted the police were informed. What happened next beggars belief and I say that as an experienced ex-cop. She was accompanied to the police office in Ayr at around 9 a.m. and was still in the station at around 11 p.m. Much later in her story, when I interviewed her in my role as an investigator of alleged injustices, she repeated what she had said from the start – while she was in the station that long day, voluntarily attending to report a rape, she suffered verbal abuse from two police officers. She was also put under pressure to retract her allegations. In addition, she told me she was denied her basic rights such as being given food, the right to use a telephone and access to legal advice.

It seems obvious to me that the intention of the interviewing officers was to get her to change her version of events so that a hard-pressed force would have one fewer case to investigate. It does nothing to excuse such behaviour to point out that, from time to time, false accusations of rape were made by people staying at the holiday camp but this was a genuine victim who voluntarily put herself into what was to become a nightmare purely to make sure her assailant did not go free.

She was driven back to the camp that night and was picked up and returned to the station at 11.30 the next morning. It appears that the pressure on her to change her story continued. The police even sent a car back to the camp to pick up a fellow employee who advised Linda to change her story and say she had not been raped. Linda refused. But the pressure continued for hours and eventually she cracked, signing a document to the effect that she had not told the truth about the rape – though why on earth she should have done so is beyond me. At 5.45 she was allowed to leave the police station.

That could have been the end of it, horrific and unsatisfactory as it was. But, no, more was to come and her nightmare grew. She was charged with 'making false accusations and wasting the time of the police' and later the might of the law took its course with this nineteen-year-old appearing at Ayr Sheriff Court. The possible consequences were dire. Her solicitor warned her that, if she went to trial and was found guilty, she could go to jail for two years. And, at the proverbial last minute, she took the less dangerous way out or so it seemed at the time. After admitting the charge, she was fined £200 and, of course, she was now a person with a criminal conviction. Interestingly, if she had insisted on going to trial, the first witness would have been the man alleged to have committed the rape. Such conflicts in court are a common occurrence in rape trials and many a victim simply can't face the ordeal of seeing their attacker face to face again.

The reader will well understand my concern about this case when looking dispassionately at the facts but some might think that the police would never have treated a rape victim in this way. That is naive. Before moving to the conclusion of Linda's story I will tell you of Susan who was also raped at Butlins in 1998. This young girl was only fifteen. She was on holiday with her parents and she was attacked on the way back to the chalet she shared with them. Like Linda, she reported the assault to the police and, like Linda, she was treated in what I would describe as a similarly inhumane way. While she was at the police station, she says she was offered no food over a period of hours and her father, who was at the station for fifteen hours, claims he was not allowed to speak to her during that period. After what she describes as aggressive questioning, Susan, like Linda, signed an admission that she had had given false information. She was allowed to leave the station and the family cut their holiday short and returned to Yorkshire.

Susan was taken to a police station in Leeds and this time interviewed compassionately. She was also examined by a doctor whose opinion was that she had indeed been raped. A DNA sample was taken and analysis of it revealed a connection to Butlins. On telling Strathclyde Police this, the Leeds cops were taken aback to be told they had no right to interfere in the case. The girl was summoned to appear at Ayr Sheriff Court but, after she travelled north on several overnight trips costing £200 a time, the procurator fiscal at Ayr informed the family that the charges had been dropped. At least Susan didn't end up with a criminal record – unlike Linda – but that was of little consolation to the family who had been forced to sell their house to pay for, among other things, all the travelling and overnight stops in Scotland.

So where do folk turn to in such circumstances? Both families sought advice from various quarters and A Search for Justice heard about the cases on the grapevine. It was all to become even more outrageous and would generate newspaper coverage in newspapers in both England and Scotland, especially in the *Sunday Mail* in Glasgow, a paper that always picks up on such stories.

Our investigations started with Linda. One day, her mum was out walking the dog and she was deep in thought about the case – she found it difficult to think of anything else at that time – and she offered up a prayer for guidance. In an astonishing piece of serendipity – I claim no otherworld guidance! – her mobile rang at that very moment. When she answered, she heard a voice say, 'Hello, my name is Les Brown and, along with a colleague, I run an organisation called A Search for Justice. Can we be of any assistance to you?'

It turned out that we could. I was able look at what had happened in-depth and the first thing I found was that, even though they didn't know each other, both girls' stories about the treatment they had received from the police matched to a remarkable degree.

Not long after Linda was fined, her parents decided to lodge an official complaint regarding the way the police had treated her. A senior detective from Strathclyde Police called at their home, which was outside the force's jurisdiction, and, according to the parents, it seemed obvious he was there to try to talk them out of continuing with the complaint. They say that, at one point, this officer told them, 'If you do not withdraw this complaint things could get very messy.' He said he was conducting an independent inquiry and claimed that the police in Ayr were 'sick and tired' of the complaints they were getting from people staying at Butlins.

The man Linda had accused was interviewed by the police and a female officer later told the family that this man had stated that he was not a drug addict. This was the first and only mention of drugs in the case.

The family also brought the matter to the attention of their MP and others but without success. A Search for Justice wrote to the Law Society on Linda's behalf, complaining about the advice her solicitor had given her before the trial. We were not too surprised by the Society's reply – the complaint, they said, was time-barred.

In 2002, we contacted all the principal players in this injustice. We went about this with the kind of compassion that seemed to be so sadly missing in Ayr. The police office in Yorkshire where the second victim had been examined and interviewed was contacted and, if the whole business had not been so tragic, I would have been amused by that phone call south. The officer I spoke to asked which force I had been in and, when I told him it was Strathclyde, he replied, 'Excuse me while I spit!' But, when he got the drift that this was a Strathclyde man chasing up the facts, he mellowed and told me I had restored his faith in human nature and proceeded to be as helpful as he could.

We also contacted an organisation called the Rape Crisis Centre. They have offices in several parts of

Scotland, including a branch in Ayr. In 1998, the year Linda and Susan claim they were raped, they said more than 1000 people has contacted them. Six men were prosecuted and four of them were found guilty – an indication of both the size of the problem and the difficulty in getting successful prosecutions.

When word of all this got out, I was contacted by other women who claimed to have been raped at Butlins. One woman told me that, months after she was attacked, she spotted the rapist and followed him to his workplace. I contacted the local police, not Strathclyde, and, after a compassionate interview with the victim, the law took its course and her attacker was jailed. We got a nice thank-you call for that one, something I really appreciated.

Years after the attack on Linda, we were not much further forward though a look back at the evidence turned up an interesting statement. According to Linda's family, back in the autumn of 1998, a female police officer told them that they would catch the rapist. This was especially interesting as this was the only admission that there had been a rape. Some years later, I interviewed this officer and she denied that she had ever uttered these words but the look on her face did not convince me.

We continued to dig deep into the case and the full extent of what happened was hard to take. For example, on the day Linda was called to the Sheriff Court, she was told to turn up at Ayr Police Station at 8 a.m. She did so and says she was then placed in a cell with others and then taken, in handcuffs, to a police van and driven to the court in time to be there for at 10 a.m. This was not normal procedure. Usually, the accused would be asked to attend the court at 9.30 a.m. and, if he or she was not present when their name was called at 10 a.m., a warrant would be issued for an arrest.

Why was Linda not accorded this treatment? Why was she made to suffer the indignity she did? Further investigation also suggested that she had been detained illegally on the two days following the rape. The Criminal Procedure (Scotland) Act 1995, Section 14(2) says, 'Detention shall be terminated not more than six hours after it begins.' This seems to have been breached in the case of Susan too.

Like the parents, A Search for Justice wondered where to go next. We met Linda's parents for a conference on the next move in this battle to right a wrong. I remembered that I had played a minor role in the original investigation of the horrific case of the Doyle Family murdered in a firebomb attack in what is now known as the Ice-Cream Wars in the east end of Glasgow. Big TC Campbell and Joe Steele were wrongfully convicted of the attack, convictions that were only overturned many, many years after the trial. Joe and TC finally got their freedom after the case went to the Scottish Criminal Case Review Commission (and after years of campaigning by some journalists and lawyers) Could this be the way forward in these cases too?

We got the appropriate forms and filled them in. On 1 December 2004, Linda opened a thick letter with the long-awaited response. The Commission wrote:

The SCCRC has now completed its inquiries into whether or not a miscarriage of justice may have occurred in respect of your conviction and sentence. The commission is not minded to refer your case to the High Court. Please find enclosed the Commission's statements of reasons for that decision.

Among the reasons given in the SCCRC's letter were some of the events leading up to the incident, including the fact that Linda had been in the company of several teenage male holidaymakers. (What's surprising about that?) Linda had never disputed this. The report went on to point out that Linda had been interviewed by two police officers, one male, one female, and that the outcome was that she was charged with making a false allegation of rape against the security guard. The Commission also noted that the applicant had not been charged with any offence on the Saturday and was at the police station voluntarily at that time. As a result of this, there was no requirement for her to have been offered the opportunity to contact a solicitor. The commission also noted that she had no entitlement to make a phone call in such a situation. It further pointed out, that in relation to what went on on the Saturday, the applicant was not being detained by the police and, because of this, there was no requirement under Section 14(2) of the Criminal Procedure (Scotland) Act 1995 for her to be released after a period of six hours. On the Sunday, the letter said, the applicant appeared to have attended voluntarily at the police station. It went on to say:

[T]he applicant was cautioned and charged at 11.34 on Sunday 24th May 1998 and released about tea time the same day. The commission is not of the view that this length of time in custody is excessive. In relation to the way the applicant was treated at the police station, she accepted that she was not handcuffed for any great length of time.

More followed in the same vein:

While the commission notes that it would have been preferable to have offered the applicant some refreshment, it is not the view that the applicant's placement in a police cell for up to two hours could be seen as excessive. The applicant's mother's complaint against the police relative to the applicant's treatment at the hands of the police, over the two days, was passed to the Procurator Fiscal at Dumfries and Galloway. No action was taken. All the police officers denied that the applicant had been subjected to any threatening or abusive behaviour. The commission is not persuaded that any alleged abusive behaviour by the male police officer on Saturday 23rd May would have influenced the applicant enough for her to retract her allegation of rape. The commission is not persuaded that the applicant may have suffered a miscarriage of justice in respect of this ground of review. The commission, in detail, reached the same conclusion in respect of the complaint against her defence team.

Well, there you are. You've read what we had to say and you've read the reply. But we didn't leave it there and, on 14 December, we responded by making the following points.

We are disappointed at your findings and your lack of investigation. Our argument has always been that Linda was forced into a situation by the police and her solicitor. Up to five minutes before entering court, she insisted to her parents she would be pleading not guilty. To say that she was not detained by the police beggars belief. On the Sunday she was charged at 11.34 a.m. and not released till teatime. Why the delay? She was not handcuffed for any great length of time? (A rape victim?) Why did she have to attend Ayr Police Office at 8 a.m. on the day of the trial?

We went on:

The police-training manual (Sect. 11, p. 19) states, 'The female should be examined by the police casualty surgeon.' We are of the opinion that Linda was intimidated by the police to such an extent that she just wanted to end the matter at the police office and later at the court. An outsider reading your report would agree with your findings and disbelieve that Strathclyde Police would treat a victim in such a manner. We would refer them to the case of Susan (not her real name) who was raped at Butlins five months later. The treatment this young girl received at the hands of the police mirrors exactly the treatment Linda received.

We also pointed out that Linda had been told that the attendance of a doctor would cost a lot of money and Susan had been told, 'Yes, we can call a doctor but it will cost £750.' During the year 1998, more than one thousand women in Scotland sought the assistance of the Rape Crisis Centre but there were only four convictions for rape that year.

Not only had we got nowhere trying to right these two apparent wrongs, it also left the problem of two alleged rapists still being at large. Linda's assailant was from abroad and can't be found. DNA could perhaps trap the vile monster who Susan says attacked her – if he could be found. But, more importantly to my mind, Linda and Susan have become two sad victims of miscarriages of justice and two reasons the police and society in general should look deeply at the way we perceive and treat the crime of rape. In such a climate, it is no wonder that so many sexual attacks go unreported and so many women have to bear the burden of a secret that they can't share and the intolerable anguish this carries with it.

5

MYSTERY IN THE SNOW

There are few places in the British Isles as bleak and dispiriting as the run-down backwaters of industrial Lanarkshire. The hinterlands round Hamilton, Coatbridge and Motherwell are depressing places these days, with gap sites galore where weeds and straggling bushes push their way up through the cracked concrete foundations of factories long razed by the bulldozers. Sub-standard housing and shops with the windows protected by corrugated iron covered in graffiti are commonplace. Once, fifty or sixty years ago, in the heyday of the steel works and mines, there was at least a commercial buzz about the place – and there was employment. But it was never a place of beauty. In the grim, cold and snowy winters of fifties, it was a hellish place to live in and to grow up in.

But one girl, Moira Anderson, never even got to do that. On a bitter winter day in 1957 in Coatbridge, she went to the local corner shop on an errand. Her grandmother had sent her out to buy some cooking fat and she was seen standing in the vicinity of a bus stop, near the shop, in swirling snow, wrapped up against the cold. She was possibly sighted getting on to a bus but, after that, she was never seen again. She simply vanished off the face of the earth, as they say, and her disappearance started one of the longest running mysteries in the history of Scottish crime. It was a disappearance that has fascinated the Scottish press for almost fifty years and, even today, there are few folk in Lanarkshire for whom the name Moira Anderson does not ring some kind of a bell. But, inevitably, the details of the story have become blurred and sometimes forgotten as the years have passed since her disappearance.

In the time since Moira McCall Anderson – to give her her Sunday name – vanished, I have served twenty-six years in the police, spent seventeen years working for the Federation Against Copyright Theft and a further four years working for A Search for Justice. In other words, it happened a long, long time ago but the sadness of the case, the public interest at the time, the mental image of a wee girl alone in the snow and a series of bizarre twists over the years have conspired to keep Moira firmly at the centre of industrial Lanarkshire's folk memory – and Glasgow's, too.

Eight years ago the publication of a book, *Where There Is Evil* (Pan), caused a sensation. In it, the author claimed her father, Alexander Gartshore, had murdered wee Moira. The author was Sandra Brown, a woman I was to get to know well. I urge you to read Sandra's book – it is an astonishing account of Moira's background, her family and her disappearance. I do not intend to dwell on the book's content in-depth – I simply want to tell the story of Moira Anderson as it emerged, step-by-step, after I was drawn into this enduring mystery as part of my work with A Search for Justice.

In April 2005, I attended a conference of a voluntary organisation called Crisis and there I met a member of the Moira Anderson Foundation who introduced me to Sandra. We had much to talk about and we also went on a walking tour of the area where Moira had disappeared. It was as grim as ever and we went to a place where Sandra believed Moira's body had been dumped by Gartshore and possibly one or two other men.

Gartshore's background was interesting to an experienced detective like myself. Some months before the Anderson case began to dominate the headlines, he had been in deep trouble with the local cops. He was accused of the rape of a twelve-year old babysitter – the girl was same age as Moira was when she disappeared – and other sexual offences. Gartshore earned his corn as a bus driver with the firm Baxter's, which ran short local services in the Coatbridge area. While the crimes he was accused of before Moira went missing had little to do with his job, that is probably far from true in the case of Moira.

For years, the authorities have taken the line that Moira's disappearance was simply a missing person inquiry. It might have been different if the cops at the time had been more on the ball. In my opinion, the word 'murder' should have replaced 'missing person'. It is incredible to discover that, although Gartshore had been locked up on the rape charge, he was actually out on bail on the day of the disappearance and driving a Baxter's bus past the stop where Moira had been seen near to the time of her disappearance. This was a man who had had been accused of raping a twelve-year-old!

He should have been a prime suspect right from the start of the hunt for the missing wee girl. But, no, the cops in Coatbridge did not twig there might possibly be a connection. It gets worse. Eventually the bus, which had been seen by witnesses around the shop at the time, came into the inquiry and the police got round to visiting the company's headquarters and speaking to the drivers and staff. Naturally, this was the talk of the area and Gartshore's wife even asked him if he had been interviewed. He told her he hadn't but that he would put that right and left the house. He returned some time later and told her that he was 'in the clear'.

Early in my 2005 inquiry, I established that Gartshore was not interviewed as a suspect at the time – he was, however, jailed for eighteen months for the rape of the babysitter.

Looking right back at the start of the case, one thing is puzzling – why would Moira go on a bus when she was almost at the shop she had been sent to by her granny? Some light was to be shed on this after the publication of Sandra's book.

Gartshore had subsequently moved to Leeds and the allegations in the book led to Detective Chief Inspector Ricky Gray of Strathclyde Police and another detective visiting him there. He, of course, denied killing Moira but did tell the investigators that she had been on his bus that afternoon. He claimed she had boarded the bus as it was her mum's birthday the next day and she wanted to go and buy her a card. I checked this out and, sure enough, the following day was Moira's mother's birthday. How did Gartshore know this? To me, a likely explanation is that he had invited Moira up to the front of the bus to talk to him and she had told where she was going and what the purpose of her journey was.

The weather was vile that day and road conditions bad – so much so, that the buses were ordered to stop running. I surmise that, on reaching the terminus, the buses unloaded the passengers and headed back to the depot. Whether Moira stayed on or got off at this point is still a vital unanswered question.

The police investigations at Baxter's tuned up a surprise. A man called James Gallogley was another of the drivers. On the surface, he was a man leading as blameless life – a pillar of so-called respectability, he appeared to be above suspicion. But this Jekyll-and-Hyde type was to be convicted of abusing five schoolgirls. In 1997, he was sentenced to ten years and this wicked man died of cancer in Peterhead. But, before he went to meet his maker and answer for his sins, he wrote a fifteen-page confession indicating that Gartshore and another man were Moira's killers. It is my suspicion that Gallogley is that other man. Intriguingly Gallogley was a married man with four children, an elder in Calder Parish Church in Coatbridge. Seemingly above reproach, he had access to young children in the Sunday School and four of his victims had grown up by the time he was arrested for interfering with a young girl. The earlier victims came forward at this time. He eventually admitted eleven charges including attempted rape and indecent behaviour. Nice friends Gartshore had.

When news emerged that I was interested in the case, the e-mails started to fly. One of Moira's sisters even got in touch from Australia and was delighted that I might shed some new light on the mystery. A retired Lanarkshire police sergeant, now in Canada, got in touch to say that, at the time of the initial investigation, a number of officers were busy painting and cleaning up the station prior to a VIP visit. I reflected that they might have been better looking at the usual suspects.

As with the rapes at Butlins Holiday Camp in Ayr that I covered in the previous chapter, I got some help from officers in Leeds. These were valuable contacts and I got in touch with them regarding Gartshore. I gave them a recent address and suggested that, since he was a convicted paedophile, it might be worth checking him out in connection with any unsolved incidents they had on their hands. They came back with news that shocked me. Gartshore, it seems, had been living with a young woman who had been found dead in the back garden, apparently having jumped from the multi-storey flat. I wonder . . .

Back in Scotland, it emerged that, before Gallogley died, he had confided what he knew about the Anderson case to a fellow inmate, who, by then, had been released and was living in Inverness-shire. There was a lot of detail in this confession. Gallogley told of Gartshore overpowering Moira with chloroform while on the bus and said that he had hidden her in a compartment in the bus which could also be accessed from the outside of the bus. My inquiries have confirmed that the bus Gartshore was driving on the day of Moira's disappearance had just such a feature. When he arrived back at the depot that fateful snowy day, Gartshore and another unknown man were said to have found that Moira had died. The unknown man was probably Gallogley and the fact that Moira had died is consistent with her being drugged and left in an unheated enclosed place in freezing Scottish weather. This ex-con said that Moira's body was dumped in an area of Coatbridge known as Witchwood Park. Anyone familiar with the area will confirm this is an ideal place to conceal a body. A stretch of ground that, in parts, is almost impossible to penetrate, it is something like a mini version of the Florida Everglades without the sun or the alligators.

As aficionados of crime fiction know, at some stage in any long-running inquiry, a mystic or medium of some sort is likely to make an appearance. I have never used them at any time in my career and take them all and their alleged mystic powers with the largest possible pinch of salt. But others disagree and some will tell you that such folk have helped solve crimes. For what it is worth, I can tell you that Sandra Brown took a well-known mystic to this muddy, bedraggled and overgrown area of Lanarkshire and that he announced, 'Moira's broken body was dumped here!' and broke down with emotion. The body, however, was never found and, even with Sandra's assistance, all my investigations were getting us nowhere. We were not helped either by announcements from the legal establishment to the effect that there is no murder without a body.

Over the years, the *Sunday Mail* had taken an interest in the case and Sandra Brown and one of their top reporters Marion Scott, who specialised in crime, went south to interview Gartshore. Both women had a right go at him but, as you might expect, he denied any involvement in the disappearance. But he threw another stone into the pond by claiming that, although he admitted Moira had been on the bus, she had left it in the company of another young girl. It was a smokescreen, of course, as no one else in the whole story has ever mentioned such a girl.

We were not making much progress but Sandra was still in touch with A Search for Justice and, in August 2005, she dropped a bombshell. She told me that a woman who owned a house and a stable near the place where Moira's body might have been concealed had found bones protruding just above the ground, adjacent to a small stream. This could be vital evidence and I was almost afraid to ask what had happened to the bones. Sandra said, 'Oh, I have them. I got them three months ago – they're in a plastic bag.' I immediately asked if anyone else knew about the bones and Sandra told me that a friend had expressed the view that they were human remains. At that moment, I had visions of Sandra being in deep trouble for hanging on to such material but I did what I had to do. One of the world's leading authorities in identifying bones is Professor Susan Black of Dundee University. She's a real expert on forensics, anatomy, anthropology and skeletal analysis and identification. When I told her what we were doing, she sounded incredulous – as well she might.

We arranged for a friend of Sandra to take the bones east to Dundee University but there was a bit of a mix-up and the bones did not arrive. However, eventually they were delivered. Much to my relief, Professor Black wasted no time phoning to say that, after examination, she was certain they were not human. If they had been, we would all have had a problem. But it looked as if the bones found at the possible dumping site were those of a dog or some other animal so now we were back to getting nowhere fast.

The next line of inquiry was to try to have a look at the police file on the disappearance and the subsequent investigation. Discreet inquires confirmed that the file was held in an office in Motherwell. I asked to have a look but formal procedure demanded that I should request access through the Freedom of Information (Scotland) Act 2002. The Strathclyde Police Disclosure Unit, based in the force's HQ in Pitt Street in the centre of Glasgow, was in charge of all requests of this kind.

I was well aware that this was a sensitive case and that the police would not be particularly happy for it to be reinvestigated for the reasons made obvious earlier in the chapter but, despite this, I applied in writing for access to the file. I did not get to see that file on the case and the official reason is bizarre to say the least. A letter told me of the refusal and I can condense its contents into one sentence – to allow access to the file you requested could be prejudicial to any ongoing inquiry. The reader will not need me to point out that, at this time, the case was nearly fifty years old and the prospects of Gartshore being brought to justice were slim to zero.

I appealed and, a couple of weeks later, a parcel was delivered to my home and I thought we were getting somewhere at last. However, the parcel didn't contain the file but newspaper cuttings on the case. And, as an indication of the lack of concern and care that had gone into this, I can tell you that one of the cuttings was on a police raid of a lap-dancing club in leafy Wiltshire.

By now, A Search for Justice was becoming expert in requesting information, under the Freedom of Information laws, on the Moira Anderson case and other cases. But Strathclyde Police were not keen on us getting files relating to unsolved murders and other crimes and our requests were rejected.

The next step in the Anderson case was to appeal to the Scottish Information Commissioner based in St Andrews. I wanted to see these files. In October 2005, I received a letter, part of which read, 'I can confirm that your request is valid in terms of the Freedom of Information (Scotland) Act 2002.' Any joy at this was short-lived. I phoned St Andrews and an official confided to me that the system was unable to cope with the demands for access. They were bogged down by appeals galore and the fact that some forces, Strathclyde in particular, were not playing their part.

All this was at the time of national furore over the shooting of the Brazilian Jean Charles de Menezes in the wake of the London tube bombings. It made me furious to read that a London reporter had used the FOI act to gain immediate access to correspondence between the Commissioner of the Met and the Home Office just hours after the terror attack. He got what he wanted and we could not get a file on forty-nine-year-old case. In April of 2006, we learned that Alexander Gartshore had died of cancer in Leeds. Scottish newspapers asked what my thoughts were on hearing the news. I said that I hoped he had died an agonising death.

This whole tale could have had a different ending if the local cops had acted with more skill originally. And if, almost fifty years later, Strathclyde had let us have the file, both Gartshore and Gallogley's old prison mate could have been interviewed and light shed on a crime that has endured in the public memory in the years since a cheery little girl headed out into the snow on a routine errand. Access to the file might now be of lesser value but, be in no doubt, it will be pursued.

6

THE GIRL WHO WENT
TO THE PUB

In my years with A Search for Justice many tormented people turned to us for help in a desperate search for peace, for what is now called 'closure'. To have had a son or daughter murdered and to live for month after month, year after year, with the uncertainty of what happened to that loved one is mental torture. Folk who have lived through such a nightmare have told me that it dominates their lives in a way that is almost inexplicable to someone who has not experienced it. One such tormented soul is Margaret Waters, mother of Tracey Waters, an eleven-year-old who died on St Valentine's Day 1983.

I felt for Margaret who, as the parents of victims often do, seemed almost to have blamed herself for the death of young Tracey. It is easy now, in the more enlightened days of the twenty-first century, to be critical but 1983 was a long time ago and life was lived to a different pattern then. What happened before the murder of Tracey was quite clear; what happened after it complex and, as such, demanding for an investigator at the time. And, if investigating Tracey's death was difficult not long after it happened, it was even more so for someone like me, trying to piece together the story more than twenty years later.

Margaret Waters came to us for help and we tried to give her it – after all, that was what our organisation, now sadly disbanded, was all about. For Margaret, it didn't matter how long ago this tragedy occurred – her search for justice was ongoing. The murder happened in Johnstone, a place, then as now, with plenty to keep a police force busy. With its mixture of well-kept bungalows, sturdy detached buildings redolent of past prosperity and many council houses, it's a rather strange little town – a place without much heart, at least to the visitor. Life in such a town back in the eighties could be bleak and dispiriting. It is not surprising then that there was something of a pub culture, especially in the less salubrious areas, and, on the night of her daughter's death, Margaret Waters had left Tracey to go for a drink in a local pub.

The eleven-year-old got bored, left the warmth of her home and wandered out into the cold February night in search of her mum who she believed would possibly be in the pub. They never met up. Tracey was found strangled behind a garage near to the pub. The grim discovery happened only hours after Margaret had returned home to find no sign of her daughter. In a state of anxiety, the mother had rounded up members of her family and they searched the area around her home and the pub with no success. This brought home the possibility of something serious having happened and all hope of Tracey being found playing or visiting a friend disappeared. Reality had to be faced and the missing youngster was reported to the local police who promptly mounted a major missing person search.

A body was found in a garden at the rear of Shanks Crescent. It had to be properly identified and, in an effort to spare her mother the pain of doing so, an uncle, Adam McDermott, agreed to help the police in the grim task. The police were later to take stick from the press and others for letting this happen when McDermott was later charged with the murder. The police were accused of lack of responsibility as this could be presented as allowing a suspect access to a crime scene. But, of course, at the stage McDermott offered his help, for apparently humanitarian reasons, he was not a suspect. Hindsight is, as they say, a wonderful thing. And I have to say clearly that, had I been investigating the murder at the time it happened, I would have done exactly what the investigating cops did. In good faith, they accepted what seemed like a genuine offer of help.

Fans of true crime and classic detective fiction are well aware of the importance of things like the footstep in the mud or snow and the state of the grass or the ground near where a body is found. Detectives these days don't wander around wearing a checked cape and with a pipe glued between their jaws and a huge magnifying glass in hand, gazing at displaced grass or gravel. However, it is undeniably true that the evidence of your eyes alone, if you look at a crime scene correctly, can help you piece together what might have happened.

And it was relatively easy for the police in the Tracey Waters case to put together a picture of what had happened. They had a witness – a man walking his dog who had seen a man running and stumbling along

Janefield Avenue away from the murder spot at about the time the crime was committed. Lone dog walkers, out at night when others are glued to the telly, do tend to see some interesting sights. The witness said he saw the man taking a route through adjoining gardens. A footprint had been left in newly dug ground and hedges, too, showed signs of a man having broken through them and, in the process crashing though the hedges, he had generally made a mess of the gardens. To me, it doesn't take much of a genius to work out that somebody would have been scratched by going through hedges like this.

Suspicion soon fell on McDermott who had been so quick to get on the right side of the cops by offering his services to identify the body. A married man with two children, he lived near Tracey Waters. He appeared to have no obvious scratches but he was arrested and charged. He spent eleven weeks in Barlinnie before being released on the instruction of the Lord Mackay, the Lord Advocate. It became a big drama with mysterious overtones. McDermott's legal team had made pleas for the charges to be dropped but without success but then Lord Mackay instructed the procurator fiscal at Paisley to order Adam McDermott to be released from jail. The precise reasons for this are not known but it was arranged. However, when the official instruction came through, it did not contain the vital words 'No further proceedings to be taken'. I have some thoughts on that later in this tale.

For eight years, McDermott continued to live locally at Kilbarchan, not far from Johnstone, but suddenly, in the late summer of 2001, he disappeared off the local radar. He was spotted visiting a post office and then he just appeared to vanish. By this time, he was divorced. He was a keen hillwalker and mountain biker who particularly enjoyed exploring the Loch Lomond area. This offered endless theories on what might have happened to him but disappeared he stayed.

Three years after this new mystery, I was approached by Tracey's mother. She told me what she knew of Tracey's death and asked me to take a look at the case. Despite the fact that it had happened in the eighties and all the problems that can arise from following a cold trail, I said I would help if I could and so began a new investigation into a chilling crime. I wanted to help Margaret who, even after all the years, was still upset at the thought that she had been the cause of her daughter leaving the safety of their home.

The close family all appeared to blame McDermott but I was not so sure. There were some things that just did not add up to a detective like me with so many years on the murder beat in Glasgow. Back to the Sherlock Holmes footprint bit. This footprint, which was found in the garden and attributed to the man the dog-walker had seen running away from the murder scene, had been made by a size ten shoe. McDermott's shoe size was seven – small for a man. It could be argued that the act of running might have made the print larger but this did not wash with me – there could have been some small difference but not the difference between a size seven and a ten.

McDermott's lack of obvious scratches seemed to me highly significant. I was also aware that, fifteen months before Tracey's death, there had been another murder – that of Pamela Hastie which is dealt with elsewhere in this book – and McDermott was not connected to this in any way.

I contacted the CID at Johnstone and, even though so many years had gone by, I was delighted to find them prepared to assist and answer all my questions – something that doesn't always happen when you approach a force about an unsolved murder on their patch. I asked if McDermott was still alive and it was established that, if he was, he was not drawing funds from any official source. The Waters Family believed that he was still alive and being supported by others. There was a theory that he was living with a woman in Helensburgh but the woman was traced and she had not seen him for years. An ex-associate of Adam McDermott calmly told me, 'He was shot and buried in a shallow grave.' He gave no more details and my suspicion is that it was not true but who knows?

I have always been very interested in the increasing importance of DNA evidence in enquiries, especially some murders and serious crimes that, in the past, did not have the advantage of the latest developments in that field. I figured DNA might have been found on Tracey's clothing and asked the Johnstone guys if that was the case. The reply was unexpected. 'As far as the DNA goes, that line of inquiry has been exhausted.' I suspected a problem and, a short time later, I put it more bluntly, asking, 'Have you got Tracey's clothing or not?' I was told, 'I can't comment – let me get back to you.'

It all became a little clearer on 13 April 2004. I was in Margaret Waters' house that day when she was visited by two senior police officers. At my suggestion, she asked if they had Tracey's clothing or not. She was told,

'No, we cannot find the clothing.' Any chance of a DNA match providing a new clue to this puzzling hard case had gone. It also sparked a thought in my inquisitive mind – could this be connected with the release of McDermott all these years ago? Was he freed when the police were instructed to lodge the productions in the case and some could not be found? Conjecture but . . .

If Adam McDermott is or was innocent, then who killed Tracey? According to Johnstone CID, there was another suspect who took a size ten shoe and who did have scratches. However, the man was able to explain these potentially incriminating things away and he was cleared – though some locals still seem to believe he was the guilty party. The man with the dog who had seen the running suspect was sure the person he'd seen was too big to be McDermott. This curious case has sparked theories galore and still holds the attention of that odd little town Johnstone and anyone with an interest in justice. Would this truly hard case ever be resolved?

Early in 2006, it was announced that a special cold case squad had been set up by Strathclyde Police. It is being led by Detective Superintendent Ken Watters, a man I know and a man respected by me and his colleagues as a dedicated and hard-working street-wise detective expected to achieve successful conclusions to a raft of difficult cases he has been given to examine. The case of Tracey Waters is on his list. I wish him well and will do anything I can to assist. For the sake of the still grieving relatives this is one case crying out for closure.

7

WHO WAS THE RUNNING MAN?

In the tale of my investigations into the death of Tracey Waters, I made some observations on the little Renfrewshire town of Johnstone, mainly on the physical appearance of the place. But, back in the early eighties, Johnstone had another characteristic – for a long time it was a place gripped by fear, haunted by the fact that two young girls had been murdered there within fifteen months of each other. People looked over their shoulders and, in homes, pubs and shopping centres, folk speculated on why it happened on their patch, whether it could happen again and, most importantly of all, who the killers were – or, indeed, if the killings were linked, who the killer was. Murder in a small community can affect everyone, not just the families of the victims. As I pointed out in the previous chapter, many question marks still hang over the death of eleven-year-old Tracey in 1983 but equally puzzling was the death of a fifteen-year-old schoolgirl, Pamela Hastie, late in 1981.

It is odd that, in a place that does not normally make the headlines, two young girls should have been murdered so close together. It is almost spooky that, in each case, a suspect had been arrested and there is now real doubt whether or not the cops had the right guy. With the possibility in my mind that there might be a link, I, nevertheless, decided to investigate the murder of Pamela Hastie separately from that of Tracey.

On a cold November day in 1981, Pamela took a decision that was to cost her her life. Walking home from school to Tower Road, Johnstone, she took a short cut through an area known as Rannoch Woods, an inhospitable and threatening spot at the best of times but an ugly place in the November gloom. She never got home. The inevitable search of likely areas for a missing body began and she was found raped and strangled in the woods.

My inquiry got an early break when I learned that the officer who had initially been in charge of the murder investigation was Detective Superintendent Jim Brown. Jim and I went a long way back, as they say, and, indeed, he had been my boss when I worked out of Cranstonhill Police Station many years before in the early days of my career as a detective. Jim had been a good boss. We worked well together and had a measure of success on the tough streets around Cranstonhill. Being able to talk to him in 2003 was a great help.

We both looked back over what had happened in Johnstone in the 1980s. In the autumn of 1981, a local youth, Raymond Gilmour, was arrested on several charges of indecent exposure. Some of the incidents were alleged to have taken place in Rannoch Woods. It is worth noting that, at this time, Gilmour was known as a 'flasher' and one of the places he would do this was in Rannoch Woods. He was such a familiar figure that it was said schoolgirls using the short cut used to wave to him in his hiding place in the bushes and have a good giggle. They were clearly unaware of the potential danger of their actions. Gilmour pled guilty to the indecent exposure offences and was placed on probation. Shortly after this, he was arrested and charged with the murder of Pamela Hastie.

In June 1982, he was found guilty and sentenced to life. By a remarkable coincidence, I was in the High Court that day as a witness in another trial. I was sitting beside Jim Brown when the verdict was declared. Brown gasped so loudly that the judge looked over to where we were sitting but the significance of that gasp of shock was only to emerge later.

Gilmour's defence team had claimed that a confession he made had been beaten out of him by the police – a common enough plea in murder cases when all else fails. Every cop knows the dangers of that game. Indeed, on one occasion, I was the victim of such a false claim. That time a murder suspect had given a voluntary statement before his solicitor arrived at the police station. When the man's legal representative did arrive, this legal eagle, in front of me and without turning a hair, calmly told his client not to worry about what he had said as 'we'll just say the statement was battered out of you'!

In the Johnstone case, Gilmour's so-called confession featured large in the legal processes that eventually got him out of jail after twenty-one years. It was riddled with inaccuracies that destroyed its credibility and it looked as if it could well have been forced out of him.

But back to my Search for Justice investigation. I knew how Jim Brown worked and beating confessions out of an accused was not his style at all. Once I'd got further into the case, I discovered something that made me think again about the confession and whether or not it was obtained by duress. It appears that, for some reason, the top men at police HQ were unhappy about the pace of Jim's investigation. They instructed Detective Chief Superintendent Charlie Craig to take over the case. Craig, now dead, was a cop of different stripe from Jim Brown and me – where we were painstaking investigators who were prepared to take our time, Craig was always a man in a hurry. He had already had a controversial career and I surmised that, once Charlie Craig was in charge and with Gilmour a strong suspect, Craig would have gone for the jugular.

I was aware that, at the time when Gilmour was brought to the police office, Brown had remarked that he, Gilmour, had a slight bruise on his face. When asked how it happened, Gilmour said that one of the officers had struck him.

But the Search for Justice inquiry turned up another remarkable piece of evidence that would work in Gilmour's favour. My co-founder Bryan Davies had heard a story in a pub about a man who was driving a hospital van past Rannoch Woods at the approximate time of the murder. This driver told of a man running from the woods and colliding with his van. The running man was knocked to the ground but he picked himself up and disappeared into the distance before the van driver could do much about it. The national and local press are always helpful in inquiries with appeals for witnesses and the like. It helps them to keep stories going and it make for good PR with police and public. And, if the press appeal turns up anything of significance, the paper can trumpet its success.

In this case, the place to start was with the popular local *Paisley Daily Express*. If we could find the van driver, it could potentially be dynamite. But this was September 2003 – more than twenty years after the murder. Were we on a wild goose chase? Apparently not! On the very day the front-page story appeared, the reporter who had written it phoned to say the van driver wanted to speak to me.

I went to see Andrew Henderson in his home and the first thing he said was, 'Mr Brown, why are you doing this?' My reply was to the effect that I was trying to find the man who had murdered Pamela Hastie. The response I got to that was, 'That'll do me – how can I help?' I took an instant liking to this guy – he struck me as a good witness and, believe me, I have had a lot of experience in this area weeding out the chancers from the real thing. Henderson was a solid witness.

What he went on to tell me and the manner he used will stay with me for a very long time. On the day of Pamela's murder he had been driving his NHS van through a T-junction adjacent to Rannoch Woods when, without warning, a man, coming from the direction of the woods, collided with the front offside of the van. For a few seconds, this man's face was pressed against the windscreen of the van, about eighteen inches from Andrew himself. There is no doubt that Andrew Henderson had a good look at the running man and he described him as aged around forty and heavily built. The man's eyes had made a particular impression on Andrew – he said they 'burned right through me'. The man was wearing a jacket with a hood and both men swore at each other about the collision before he moved off. One thing was certain – this was not Raymond Gilmour.

I listened to all this and then asked Andrew whether he thought he would know the man if he saw him again. The reply was chilling. He claimed, 'Yes, I have seen him again since that day – on television. The man who ran into my van was Robert Black.' He elaborated on this and explained how, years later, he had been watching TV with friends and a news programme showed a prisoner being escorted into a prison van. He immediately exclaimed to his friends that the man on the screen was the man who ran into the van. The man on the news was Robert Black, the infamous child killer. Black, a lorry driver from England, had been convicted of murdering three young girls and attempting to abduct another. He is serving life with a minimum of thirty-five years and, since his conviction, Black has kept making headlines and has been linked with as many as fifteen other child murders in six countries.

The next part of the story made unpleasant listening. The day after the collision with the running man, Andrew had taken his van to the police command vehicle where the inquiry was being coordinated and told the cops there what had happened the day before on the edge of Rannoch Woods. He suggested that, since the running man had placed both hands on the bonnet of the van, it might be possible to obtain fingerprints from it. Amazingly, this obvious suggestion was ignored.

Telling me all this brought back memories for Andrew and he became visibly upset. He explained that he felt

In 2001, the body of Invernesian Innes Ewart was found below a multi-storey car park in Stratford, London. The police said it was suicide but there was nothing in this successful young man's life to suggest he would have jumped to his death. ('Fatal Falls and Police Flaws')

Kevin McLeod was looking forward to his wedding day but one Friday night, in 1997, after going out for a few drinks with a friend in Wick, he never made it home. ('Fatal Falls and Police Flaws')

Kevin's body was found on the seabed here at Wick Harbour. His death was accidental, according to the police, but the fact that several people testified to Kevin having been assaulted during the evening might have had a bearing on how he really died.

This is the lay-by near Erskine Bridge where prostitute Jacqueline Gallagher's body was found, wrapped in a curtain, in 1996. ('Life and Death on the Streets')

Witnesses reported something that looked like a rolled-up carpet being dragged from a red Citroën van like the one in this picture. Chief Inspector Jeanette Joyce also holds up curtain material similar to that wrapped around Jacqueline.

Jacqueline Gallagher's mother, Alice Wilson (wearing glasses), and Jeanette Joyce hold a press conference one year after Jacqueline's body was found, in the hope that new information will surface about who Jacqueline's killer might be.

Here are two contrasting pictures of Emma Caldwell. One shows her before the impact of her sister's death sent her life spiralling out of control. In the other, her beautiful face has been ravaged by her years of heroin addiction and working as a prostitute.

And this is Emma not long before her body was found dumped in a remote area near Biggar in May 2005. ('Life and Death on the Streets')

For thousands of Scots, a visit to Butlins in Ayr brought nothing but happy memories but, in 1998, a trip to the holiday camp ended in a hellish experience for two teenage girls. ('Hell in a Holiday Camp')

The logo of the Moira Anderson Foundation, a charitable organisation set up in Moira's name to support victims of child sex abuse.

On a bitter winter day in 1957 in Coatbridge, Moira Anderson went a message to the local shop. She was never seen again. ('Mystery in the Snow')

This is Alexander Gartshore with his daughter Sandra. In her book, *Where There Is Evil*, Sandra Brown claims that her father was responsible for killing Moira. Sandra is the driving force behind the Moira Anderson Foundation.

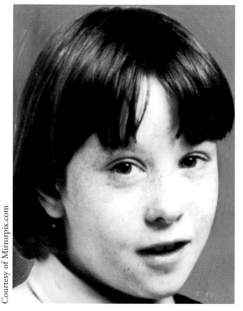

On the evening of Valentine's Day 1983, eleven-year-old Tracey Waters left the warmth and safety of her home to find her mum who had popped out for a drink at a local pub in Johnstone. Tracey never quite made it to the pub – her strangled body was found nearby. ('The Girl who Went to the Pub')

Tracey's uncle, Adam McDermott, wanted to spare her mother the anguish of having to identify Tracey's body so he volunteered to do it. He was later charged with Tracey's murder and spent eleven weeks in jail before the charges were dropped. Eight years later, McDermott disappeared and has never been heard of since.

Margaret Waters visits Tracey's grave twenty years after she died. She sought the help of A Search for Justice in finding out what happened to her daughter.

On a cold November day in 1981, an impetuous decision to use a short cut home from school was to cost fifteen-year-old Pamela Hastie her life. She was found raped and strangled in Rannoch Woods, not far from where Tracey Waters' body was discovered. ('Who Was the Running Man?')

Although Raymond Gilmour was convicted of Pamela's murder, he was released after an appeal. Some believe that this man, convicted child-killer Robert Black, was actually responsible. He was, however, cleared of any connection to the killing and the case remains unsolved.

Les Brown gives Margaret Milne, a well-known Glasgow reporter, an update on a murder investigation he was involved in during his time with the Serious Crime Squad. He has always believed in the usefulness of the media in the gathering of information.

This birthday boy and avid Celtic supporter is John Kidd. John was out playing football at his local park in Dundee when he was attacked by a gang. He died from his injuries but, had the police reacted more quickly to an emergency call from neighbours, there's a chance he might have survived. ('The Van that Never Was')

Norman Whittle looks completely distraught and no wonder – who would have believed that a visit to a car boot sale, in 2004, would have concluded in a fight over a parking space which left his wife Ann dead? ('Death at the Fruit Market')

Carol McMillan is ushered away from court by a friend after being given probation and community service for causing the death of Ann Whittle. A later appeal saw this sentence increased to four years in custody, still some way short of the ten years Ann's family believed McMillan deserved.

In 1976, Renee McRae and her three-year-old son Andrew disappeared. Renee's BMW was found burnt-out in a lay-by on the A9, just south of Inverness. She had been on her way to meet her lover in Perth. ('What Lies Beneath the A9?')

Farmer Brian McGregor marks the spot where he believes Renee's and Andrew's remains might lie. Brian has spent a large amount of his own money trying to find out what happened to this mother and son.

If our mum's death was just an accident, what happened to the £2000 in her purse?

Family believe gran was killed

Our mum: With Bryan and wife Lesley

Courtesy of Mirrorpix.com

EXCLUSIVE
By MARION SCOTT

THE distraught family of a granny found dead in her home believe she was murdered by a thief who stole £2000 from her handbag.

Police investigating the death of sprightly Annie Davies, 84, say she died after falling downstairs.

Now her relatives are taking legal action to prove she was murdered after a policeman told them: "Your mum was robbed and murdered. But I'm not in charge of the case."

Annie's blood-spattered body was found lying behind the front door of her first-floor, main-door flat at Ayton Drive, Erskine, Renfrewshire, on May 30, 1998.

Mistake

Her cheekbone was smashed, her jaw was broken and there were bruises on her back. A pathologist concluded that the force of one or more blows dislodged Annie's dentures and she choked to death.

Strathclyde Police assured her family death was an accident. But within hours, the family found clues which pointed to Annie having been brutally battered.

Her son Bryan, 53, noticed Annie's purse containing £2000, her handbag and keys had vanished.

"That was when we realised, this was no accident. There is only one explanation. Mum was murdered for her money," Bryan said.

"Someone forced their way in, beat her to a pulp and fled with her bag and purse. I'm convinced that as long as police are embarrassed to admit a mistake, a murderer is free and other pensioners are at risk."

Brother Fred, 54, told how his

THE SUNDAY MAIL INVESTIGATES

mother carried around large sums of money. He said: "Mum kept her savings in her handbag. She'd only go to the bank when we chided her."

Bryan and Fred think Annie's murderer knew she would have large sums of money in her flat.

They were stunned when police ruled the death accidental, despite a post-mortem report revealing Annie had sustained "one or possibly more blows" and "severe blunt force injuries to her face." The report said assault could not be ruled out.

CID officers told the family Annie had slipped and smashed her cheekbone on a kitchen unit and began to choke on her dentures. They say her injuries were caused when she fell downstairs, on her way to get help.

They cannot explain why she ignored a panic button in her hall.

Or why, since she suffered from osteoporosis, or brittle bones, there were no fractures to her limbs, or injuries to the front of her body.

The family believe her broken cheekbone was caused by the front door being slammed into her face.

They believe the bruises found on her face, shoulders and spine are consistent with being thrown back on to the stairs and held down while her attacker repeatedly punched her.

Gloves

The family say police told them hand prints on Annie's front door were left by paramedics. But Bryan says he watched the paramedics putting on rubber gloves before they went near the door.

Family lawyer Manus Tolan said: "I'm baffled that this was not treated as suspected murder from the start."

The family have been refused a fatal accident Inquiry, and the assis-

tant procurator fiscal involved, Dr David Griffiths, has told them: "My involvement with Mrs Davies's unfortunate death is now concluded. This decision is final."

Strathclyde Police refuse to discuss the case. A spokesman said: "The circumstances were fully investigated and reported to the fiscal."

MP Tommy Graham, who has spent months writing to the authorities on the family's behalf, said: "I believe this family deserve a proper inquiry. I won't stop asking questions until this is achieved."

● If you have information, contact Marion Scott on 0141 242 3239.

Fated to die: Smiling granny Annie Davies was the victim of a horror accident – or a murderous burglar

Courtesy of Mirrorpix.com

The police seemed determined that Annie Davies' death was as a result of her having fallen down the stairs at her home in Erskine in 1998. The fact that a significant sum of money and her house keys were missing didn't seem to concern them at all. ('The Body Behind the Door')

Bryan Davies outside his mum's house. Bryan's resolve to find out what really led to his mother's death was behind him co-founding A Search for Justice. Although now disbanded, the organisation helped many families seeking to know more about the crimes their loved ones had fallen victim to.

Courtesy of Mirrorpix.com

he could have done more at the time of the murder. I pointed out he had properly reported the matter and given the police access to the van to look for prints. He was blameless. What else could he have done? Nothing. But, nonetheless, Andrew Henderson said to me, 'If it was Robert Black, these other murders could have been prevented.'

We went on to talk further and I said I had to point out that now everyone knew about Robert Black and his murderous activities he, Andrew, might be accused of jumping on a bandwagon when he claimed a similarity between the running man and Black all these years later. With another remarkable disclosure, he seemed to blow that notion out of the water right away and he also showed just how reliable a witness he was. He told me that if I checked with the police, I would find that, a few weeks after the murder, he had been asked to help produce an identikit picture of the running man. He asked me to compare the picture he produced with Black's picture.

Naturally, I went to the cops about this and they confirmed that there had been such an identikit made but now they were unable to find it! I have, however, to say that identikits are subject to wide variation and can prompt incorrect identification. Remember the famous Bible John poster? The lives of dozens of innocent folk who did bear striking resemblances to the image were thrown into turmoil. The likeness to the poster was so strong in these cases that neighbours or workmates reported them to the police.

In the midst of all this I telephoned Jim Brown at his home for another natter on the case. I got straight to the point and asked if he thought Raymond Gilmour had murdered Pamela Hastie. My old boss was unequivocal and said, no, he didn't and this was from the officer initially in charge of the investigation. When I asked him if he had a particular reason for this stance, he then made some telling points. One of them was that Pamela's body was found at a spot thick with the plants known as sticky willies. Jim told me that everyone who attended the scene was covered in the little sticky balls that come off the plants and cling on to your clothes. Days later, cops were still picking sticky willies off their uniforms. There was no trace of this on Gilmour's clothing or in his house or anywhere else he had been.

I went on to ask Jim if he was aware a witness had come forward on the day of the murder claiming that a man, running from the direction of the Rannoch Woods at the material time, had collided with his van. Jim Brown replied that he could recall the incident and that some of the detectives working on the case thought this running man was a viable suspect. All this begs the question: why was this lead not followed up? Jim Brown told me I would need to ask others that question. Finally, I asked if, at a later date, it had ever been suggested that the running man was Robert Black. The answer was no.

In addition to Jim Brown, I spoke to other retired senior detectives who had worked on the case. They could recall the running man colliding with the van and remembered that they had called him the 'puffing man'. It seems incredible now that this line was not followed up. One reason was obviously that Gilmour had come into the frame and other suspects were not investigated thoroughly enough. To me, it seems like what you might call a rush to injustice.

There was yet another surprising development to crawl out of the woodwork in this more-than-twenty-year-old tale. The local newspaper now had the bit between its teeth and was covering the investigations, new and old, in-depth. They gave me the name and telephone number of a woman and suggested I contact her. This woman told me that, at the time of the murder, she worked for a voluntary organisation and, in this role, she spoke to a woman seeking advice on a matter that had been troubling her. This woman claimed that, on the day Gilmour was convicted, she had gone to the Paisley police to tell them he was innocent. She said she had picked up a man at a pub on the night of Pamela's murder and she had awakened during the night to find him in tears. When she asked what the matter was, he told her he had 'killed that girl in the woods'.

This was not what the police would want to hear on the day of what was, from their viewpoint, a successful conviction. Officially, the crime had been solved and Gilmour was the perpetrator. I tried my best to trace this woman but without success. However, the publicity was turning up other interesting facts. I was told that Robert Black and other lorry drivers used a bed-and-breakfast establishment near a Johnstone bowling club at the time of the murder. I was quickly on the streets and, being a keen bowler myself, I soon found the club and, sure enough, opposite it was a two-storey building with a wrought-iron black railing across the front. It was the place described in the tip-off.

I knocked on the door and a young man confirmed that, at one time, it had indeed been a B&B used by long-distance lorry drivers. As we chatted, another local appeared and said that he recognised me as the man investigating the Pamela Hastie murder. He went on to say that the infamous Robert Black had used the place and had, on occasion, gone over to the bowling club for a drink with the other drivers. I concealed my astonishment and asked how he knew this about Black. I was told that it was common knowledge. I went across the road to the club and saw a guy I knew to be a fellow indoor bowler. He and others confirmed that Robert Black used to drink there.

At the time of the Johnstone murders, Black worked as a van driver delivering posters to addresses all over the UK. After his conviction, the police reopened numerous unsolved murder inquiries. In his job driving around Britain, he had to keep his receipts for petrol and these chits are invaluable in placing Black in certain areas of the country and proving the dates he was there. I passed all the information gleaned from my Search for Justice inquiry to Detective Chief Superintendent Roger Orr, of Lothian and Borders Police. He was the Scottish arm of a consortium of international senior detectives engaged in the task of looking at unsolved murders and I hoped my information would help him discover if Black could be connected to any of them.

The reply I got from Mr Orr was pretty unequivocal – they ruled out Black having been anywhere near Johnstone at the time of the murder. So that appears to be that and now there is no doubt that the mystery man who ran from the woods remains just that – a mystery man.

Another piece of interesting information I discovered was that a noted psychologist, Ray Wyre, had interviewed Black after he had been convicted. I phoned him and he was cooperative. He had talked to Black over a period of years but this hugely evil man would not discuss any case he had not been convicted of and flatly refused to help the police. You would imagine that, if you were asked about cases in which you were not involved, you would simply say so. Incidentally, Wyre was of the view that Black could have been responsible for the murders of fifteen or more children.

This intriguing case of Raymond Gilmour caught the eye of TV and an excellent Channel 4 programme *Trial and Error* proved beyond doubt that this was an unsafe conviction. Interestingly, the owner of the B&B establishment I had traced appeared on the programme with another titbit. At the time of the Pamela Hastie murder, one of the guests had cut off his hair with a pair of scissors and departed the establishment early despite the fact that he had paid in advance and was still owed another night. And another perhaps significant bit of evidence came to me later. It included a report that Black had a pal in Johnstone in the ice-cream van business – what easier way to mix with young kids?

In August 2002, Raymond Gilmour was freed on parole, pending an appeal, following an investigation by the Scottish Criminal Cases Review Commission. Up to this point, his continuing insistence of his innocence had cost him any chance of parole. His appeal is still pending. My own opinion is that the man who killed Pamela

Hastie is the man, whoever he was, who collided with the van driven by Andrew Henderson. I am convinced of the innocence of Raymond Gilmour. Charlie Craig is dead but one thing is at least clear – the bonnet of Andrew Henderson's van should have been tested for prints.

8

SERIOUS RETAIL REFRESHMENT – FREE

There is a rather chauvinist joke about where a woman goes when the going gets tough. A trip to major-league shops, a hit on the husband's credit card, a nice cup of tea and a journey home festooned with shopping bags sporting upmarket logos can work wonders. Retail refreshment is powerful medicine and I suppose it does work. But, for the detective, shopping or, in his case, shoplifting can turn up interesting cases where the customer takes a trip to the stores and leaves well refreshed with no money changing hands. And here I am not talking about little old ladies who nick a tin of ham off the bottom shelf of a corner shop. There are 'super shoplifters' and large shoplifting gangs who, despite specialising in non-violent crime, can sometimes be as ingenious and as hard to catch as some of their more ruthless brethren.

But it has to be admitted that many shoplifters are well known to the cops and sometimes it is far from a hard case to nab them. A classic example was a guy called Shorty who turned out to be better known to the police than even a naturally suspicious copper like myself would believe possible. He was a regular criminal who was lifted for all sorts of minor offences, including shoplifting.

On one occasion, he had been arrested by cops in the Shawlands area and, having heard of me, he told the desk cops he wanted to speak to me. I turned up not knowing quite what to expect but Shorty said he wanted a favour. He told me that, if I had the power to release him there and then, he would return to the police station voluntarily the next morning – guaranteed. I was shocked when he told me the reason it was so important that he got out that night. He said he was needed to play on the left wing of a police football team. Apparently he had mates in the Tobago Street Police Station team and they had a particularly important match on that night.

Slightly gobsmacked, as they say, I called the duty officer at Tobago Street and he said they did have a big game on that night, against another police side. I mentioned Shorty and was told he was one of their stars – a wizard on the left wing. He was not released and the team, minus their best player, was beaten. It amazed me that such a criminal was mixing socially with police officers. It adds a whole new dimension to the phrase 'known to the police'!

Shorty's pals in blue must have been going around with their eyes half shut for, in his latest escapade, he was involved in some serious action. We discovered that he was selling very expensive-looking rings at a fraction of their apparent true value. We listened to what was being said on the streets and turned up enough info to allow us to intercept a car containing Shorty and a few cronies, all active criminals. I had a look at one of the rings and it seemed pretty impressive to me but, as I was no gems expert, I took it to Laing's, a long-established and much respected jewellery store in the city. A member of the family who owned the store, Stuart Laing, offered to do a valuation himself. At first glance, he thought it might be worth more than £5000 but, as it was the CID asking the questions, he took a more careful, considered look and found that the ring was not what it appeared to be. It was zircon in a genuine valuable gold setting. We traced the rings back to a totally legitimate south-side jeweller who had sold them to Shorty at the proper price, unaware that his customer wanted them to pass off as genuine diamond rings and sell them at a considerable profit.

This was bad news for potential customers and bad news for the jewellery trade as well. Stuart Laing went on national television news to warn the public about the scam. It is an interesting fact that, since Shorty was known to many as a crook, the buyers of his rings thought they were getting stolen property of high value at a bargain price. It says something about greed I suppose. We chased up a few of the folk who had been fooled. One publican in Edinburgh, not on Shorty's patch, paid five grand each for two rings! He denied it but it was obvious that Shorty, that demon of the football field, had scored again and conned him.

Shorty's shoplifting was not in the league of the five-quid Marks and Sparks bra snatcher but it was not quite in the league of a smart cookie I will call Tam either. Tam got me into a lot of bother (any young cops reading this take note!).

A colleague, Detective Superintendent Davie Frew, rang me to tell me that diamonds worth £25,000 had been stolen from a store at Anderston Cross. There was a real mystery about how the thief could have got his hands on the sparklers – they had been on display under a glass-topped counter secured by six screws. To get at the jewels, the thief would have to have removed each of the screws without any of the staff noticing – unless, that is, it was an inside job and the screws had been loosened or someone was determined not to notice them being removed.

Smart cookie or not, Tam had been spotted in a car park at the rear of the store around the time of the theft and Davie Frew told me that Tam and his common-law wife, a prostitute, had been lifted at their home. One of them was taken to the Turnbull Street office and the other was whisked off to Cranstonhill.

Tam was being difficult and denying being involved so Davie, aware that I knew him, asked if I would help. It is surprising at times how strong the bond between low-life couples can be. Tam was annoyed that his 'wife' had been dragged into the investigation and said, if she was released, he would admit the theft of the rings. The cops let her go and I told her to phone Tam from their home to confirm what had happened, which she did. Tam then said he would return the rings on the condition no one else got involved. He said, 'It was me who stole them and I'll plead guilty to that in court but only if you keep your word.'

Davie and I discussed the deal on offer with some others. We agreed with Tam's request that no one else would get involved so long as we recovered the rings

– after all, without them, there was no case. Detective Sergeant Brian Laird and I went to an address Tam had given us – a high-rise place in Roystonhill. We were let in by a female I had never seen before who was in a wheelchair. Tam's wife joined us and was told to produce 'the stuff'. She left the house and returned ten minutes later with a bag containing diamond rings with the price tags still attached (Shoplifters like to do this so that customers for their stolen merchandise know the real price.) I counted out the rings and there were seventeen. I told Tam that the shop had claimed more than seventeen had been taken. 'They are at it,' said this experienced crim.

When we took the stolen jewels back to Davie at Turnbull Street, he thanked us and then Brian and I made statements about exactly what had happened. Some weeks later we had to attend the procurator fiscal's office at Custom House Quay for a precognition (a legal statement taken in advance of possible legal proceedings) before the upcoming trial. The fiscal took me through my statement to clarify any points that might come up in court and the same was done with all other witnesses in the case. It was no surprise when I was asked to name the householder in whose home the rings had been handed over but, remembering my agreement with Tam, I refused to do so. As I said, I did not know her, never mind know her name. But, to tell the truth, I could have got it if I'd tried – the voters' roll, for example, would have provided the info. The fiscal insisted but I told him what had happened and that I had given my word. Not good enough was the response.

I had made a dangerous mistake. Two weeks later a letter arrived from the Crown Office in Edinburgh instructing me to name the householder and again I refused. It seems I was now not onside with the fiscal's department. Incidentally, I was never convinced that Tam, although he admitted stealing the rings, had managed to magically remove the six screws without detection – I doubt if even David Copperfield could have done that. It seemed of some significance that Tam was a bit of a ladies' man and all the assistants in the store were female – a little help from his friends?

The trial was a sheriff and jury affair and Tam, on seeing who the sheriff was, said that he had appeared before him a couple of times before. He told us that, if we could arrange another court that day, he would definitely plead guilty. He was firmly told that was not on so he pled not guilty and went to trial. Well aware that a lot of people were unhappy about my involvement in the case, I had a long talk with Brian while we were waiting to be called. I told him that, if he had any problems when giving evidence, he should stick to the truth and not attempt to protect anyone. In this, I included those present that day in the high-rise in Roystonhill where the jewels were recovered.

When I went into the box, the procurator fiscal took me through my statement and mentioned the fact that I had been asked to assist in questioning Tam because I had had previous dealings with him and, because of that, he trusted me. The fiscal asked me, 'What was the first question you asked the accused at Turnbull Street police office?' I answered that I asked if he had stolen the rings. I was then asked what he replied and, truthfully, I said that, *at that stage*, he had replied to the effect that he had not stolen the rings. The fiscal did not seem to get any inference out of this and looked puzzled. To be helpful I added that the interview had lasted over an hour – I hoped this would indicate that Tam had finally admitted the theft but only after his 'wife' had been released. After a few more questions, the fiscal sat down, still looking puzzled.

Tam's solicitor, Len Murray, one of Glasgow's legendary pleaders, stood up and addressed me. 'Could someone other than my client be responsible for the theft of the rings from the display stand?' he asked.

'Yes,' I replied as I still didn't see how he could have got at the rings without help.

I went back to work and was astounded to get a call from Tam thanking me for getting him off! He then went on the make some derogatory remarks about the brainpower of the fiscal who, according to Tam, didn't get what I was trying to tell him. It was another example of what can happen giving evidence in court where you are limited in what you can say and can only respond to the questions you are asked. If the cross-examiner does not ask the right questions, the truth can unintentionally be obscured.

I was in some bother, though, because the outcome of the case was that the fiscal sent a letter of complaint to the chief constable, saying that, in effect, I had deliberately misled the court. It meant a trip to HQ for me to attend a meeting with Assistant Chief Constable Willie Cant who informed me of the complaint and warned me that, from then on, I would need to be ultra vigilant as the prosecuting service would be monitoring my cases carefully. I had already figured that that might be the case!

Fans of the movies and TV will be familiar with the use of stake-outs by the police – a procedure where a house or office where criminality is suspected is watched over 24/7 by squads of detectives. Although it does happen, it is not a technique that is used in humble shoplifting cases very often. However, I remember using it once in the case of a shoplifting team led by a guy I call Bernard. Nowadays a lot of shoplifting is done by young women stealing to finance their drug habits but, back in my days on the streets, money was the simple motive.

Organised gangs, snatching in bulk from city shops, could make a lot of cash. Bernard was the top gun in a well-organised team working mostly from the Saracen area of the city. Informers are vital to detectives and we had our own sources, as they say. Hints we were getting indicated that a well-known criminal on the other side of the town from Saracen, in douce Dennistoun, was buying big time from the shoplifting gangs and moving the stuff on at a tidy profit.

Along with a colleague, Woman Detective Constable Janet Grant, I took a stroll along the street where the resetter lived. We quickly noticed that, immediately opposite the suspect's address, there was a flat for sale. Great – it was going to be just like the movies! Janet went to the local estate agents and got the keys and we moved in. There are jokes galore about what goes on behind the lace curtains of such flats in respectable areas but the shenanigans in this case amounted to Janet and me hiding behind the curtain armed with binoculars.

After a few hours' wait, sure enough, along came a car to stop outside the suspect's address. Out struggled six men – one of them Bernard. As we secretly watched, all sorts of items were unloaded from the boot and they disappeared up the close. That was good enough for us – we would do some more observation and perhaps raid the place the next day.

After a night's sleep, we were on the way back to our stake-out when we saw a car parked outside a shop in London Road. The vehicle was known to be used for the resetting of stolen goods so we stopped our car, searched the parked car and duly found a haul of stolen stuff. We paused on our way to Dennistoun and saw to it that the two guys who had been in the car were locked up.

When we got to Dennistoun, we saw the same car as we had seen the previous day outside the suspect's house but, before we could make a move, five men appeared out of the close-mouth, jumped into the car and drove off. We gave chase close behind and called for help on the blower. A traffic squad car overtook us and pulled the car we were chasing into the side of the road. One of the occupants was so quick off the mark that he escaped but we lifted the rest including Bernard. The traffic guys who had helped us to nab them took them off to Tobago Street and we went back to Dennistoun.

I knocked on the door of the house we'd been watching and a female asked who was there. 'Bernie,' I replied and the door opened. We walked into the living room where the owner, his son and two other men sat chatting. On a coffee table in front of them, we saw a tray of diamond rings, three obviously very expensive wristwatches, a gold cigarette lighter and more than £100 in notes. But there was more to be found in this Aladdin's cave – a search of the place turned up two leather jackets, a fur coat, three gents' suits, a portable TV and three valuable rugs. In the time-honoured fashion of the fence, all the goods had the original price tags dangling from them.

You do get a laugh or two in the police force and I could barely suppress one when the owner of the house nodded me aside and, once he'd got me on my own, he whispered to me, 'Is there anything I can do to square this?' Plead insanity was my advice.

Right after this, another thief landed in our lap when a knock on the door was answered and in walked a youth carrying a typewriter. It was replaced with handcuffs.

But there was yet another surprise in store for us back at Tobago Street. The men we had arrested on the way to Dennistoun turned out to part of Bernard's gang. They were all charged with being known thieves and associates of known thieves and detained to appear at the magistrate's court the following morning. We believed that they would be remanded there for a couple of days giving us enough time to have some of the recovered property identified. Some of it was easy – the rings had been stolen from a shop in Irvine and the portable TV from a shop in Dunfermline. Some of the other stuff was also traced to the original owners.

But sometimes things don't go quite to plan and, despite the fact that we now had evidence to charge them with theft of the recovered goods, the fiscal at the court did not ask for a remand and the accused were allowed to walk free. They were cock-a-hoop when they heard they were to be released and that they would be dealt with at a Sheriff Court later. However, I wasn't happy at all. I decided to line them up at the uniform bar of the Central Police Office and told the whole bunch of them that they were being charged with conspiring together to commit the crime of theft by shoplifting. There was a stunned silence – they just could not believe what they were hearing. Even the duty officer looked impressed and told me he had never heard of such a charge. But it worked. They were detained and appeared at the Sheriff Court the same day on petition and bail was refused. Suddenly this crew were in deep trouble, a simple shoplifting case had escalated into something more serious and complex.

Colleagues told me that they had never heard of such a charge and I stirred it up a bit by saying, 'Neither have I!' But the case went to a Sheriff Court with a jury and I gave evidence for almost all of the first day of a two-day trial. Despite the defence lawyer getting it into his head that the police were lying and that the stake-out had never taken place, all of the accused were found guilty. They were referred to the High Court for sentence. The resetter got five years, which was reduced on appeal to four, and the others received varying sentences, the maximum of which was three years, so it was quite a result for us.

Of course, it is much more usual to find shoplifting being done by the individual – one desperate person trying to smooth the path of a difficult life. And they mostly get caught, their very desperation making them take chances and not think through the risk of detection. It is sad for often a lot of the stuff they get caught nicking is of little value.

One lone regular was a woman called Sadie. She was hardly the type to disappear into the background of the wealthy fur-coated ladies of Bearsden and the leafy south-side suburbs who were the core clients of the famous old Sauchiehall Street store, Daly's. And she was spotted there, looking out of place, one day around the time a ring or two disappeared. I knew Sadie of old and was asked to have a word with her and I did. She confessed and returned the rings. With her serial record for shoplifting, she could have been jailed but I put in a good word for her and she was fined. Was she grateful? I ran into her in town a few weeks later and she took a look at me carefully and asked what size of suit I took, remarking at the same time I looked 'a forty-four'. I declined the offer.

9

DEATH AT THE FRUIT MARKET

If there is one lesson to be learned by anyone who is ever involved in a search for justice or, indeed, embroiled in a truly hard criminal case of any kind it is that you need strength of purpose, patience, energy, total belief in your cause and the ability to fight on and on despite setbacks. Justice in Scotland, it seems, is not handed out on a plate and, as this book shows many times, there are occasions when what happens in the courts flies in the face of common sense. It is heartening, however, to note that justice can often be achieved after a long fight and many dark days when a positive outcome seemed impossible. No case demonstrates all this more fiercely than the story of the death of fifty-eight-year-old grandmother Ann Whittle. I became involved when her family, who are fulsome in their praise of the police if not what happened in the courts, asked me to assist in an approach to the Criminal Injuries Compensation Board, which I did.

There are two remarkable things about Ann's death – where it took place and the public nature of it. Glasgow's fruit market is in Blochairn and it does exactly what it says on the tin – it provides excellent facilities for fruit growers, farmers, importers etc. to sell every imaginable type of fruit and vegetable. Around dawn from Monday to Saturday, it is a hugely bustling place with buyers and sellers using their wits to make a living. Amid the sweet scent of fresh fruit, there is a hint of the more robust smell of traders chasing a profit. I liked the atmosphere of the place when I used to visit during my days with the Federation Against Copyright Theft though it was mostly on a Sunday when I called. With the big time fruit merchants enjoying a day off, the area was then turned into a cross between the famous Barras and a car boot sale. Pirate DVDs and CDs were not much to be seen in this market, which was mostly legitimate but I had one amusing morning there when the police took away a stallholder for a chat. I was left in charge of his stuff and took his place selling the goods. I did a fair bit of business, as I thought, but, when I gave stallholder the takings on his return, he turned up his nose at the fifty quid I handed over. In his view, the stuff I sold was worth nearer five hundred! Maybe I should have paid more attention to the commercial world in my earlier days.

The police were always about such a busy market and their presence meant that there was normally very little trouble, few thefts or assaults but, one day in August 2004, there was to be a dramatic and tragic exception to the rule. The fruit market was ideal for its Monday to Saturday role but, on Sundays, there was a major drawback – not enough parking for the hundreds who like to throng the place searching for bargains. What happened that day and later in the High Court was to highlight the shortcomings of the legal system in

Scotland. It all began with something we are all familiar with – two cars making for the same parking space at roughly the same time. Although it is a familiar scenario, it is not usually one that results in violent death.

What happened next on that August day in the fruit market was as disgusting as it was astonishing. Ann Whittle had left her husband Norman's car and was in the process of guiding him into a space that was becoming vacant. As she did so, Norman was impeded when Carol McMillan, a thirty-four-year-old from Holytown in Lanarkshire, placed her hands on the bonnet to prevent him moving into the space. This was clearly done in an effort to let her partner, Charles Freeburn, also in his mid thirties, get to the space first as his car was nearby. This was bad enough – a touch of what you might call parking space rage – but what happened next was completely out of the box. A verbal argument about ownership of the parking slot took place and, during it, Carol McMillan pulled Ann's hair and kicked her about the head three times as she crouched on the ground. Onlookers said McMillan's face was contorted with rage and she seemed to have gone berserk.

Ann Whittle collapsed and died of a heart attack, there and then, as a result of the ferocious assault. In the midst of all this mayhem, her husband Norman attempted to come to her aid but witnesses say he was physically prevented from doing so by Freeburn. Bear in mind that this was all being watched by hordes of Sunday afternoon shoppers and some of them saw McMillan, obviously aware of what she had done, using her mobile to dial 999. During this call, she reported to the police that she had been assaulted rather than the other way round. The horrific incident was also seen by two security men who were prevented from coming to Ann Whittle's aid by a high security fence between them and the car park.

The police were quickly on the scene and witnesses ran to tell them what had happened. McMillan was arrested, charged with Ann's death and detained. The trauma of what had started as a quiet day out in the sun must have been horrendous for her husband Norman. Indeed, when I met him almost two years later in Baird Street Police station to discuss the case and how I could help, he still seemed far from fully recovered. Two days after the death in the car park, on 17 August 2004, Carol McMillan appeared in court charged with murder. Her next appearance was on 3 May 2005 when she pleaded guilty to the lesser charge of culpable homicide. On the very same day, there was another blow of fate for Norman Whittle when his son Craig, aged thirty-five, died from a fall as a result of an epileptic seizure.

Life was already dealing Norman Whittle, a retired builder, a hard hand but it was to get even worse. A couple of months later, Carol McMillan walked free from Dunfermline High Court, having being sentenced by the presiding judge, Lady Dorrian, to probation and community service. The media storm was enormous – it was a verdict that shocked the whole of Scotland. One comment from Lady Dorrian annoyed me particularly – at one stage in the case, she remarked that there was not much chance of McMillan repeating this crime. Oh, really? So that's OK, then. The papers, the TV reporters and anyone who had followed the sensational case were all entitled to ask the question, 'How can this be justice?'

On the day after the sentencing, the family urged the Crown to appeal against what was obviously a hugely lenient sentence and they started a petition that eventually had around 30,000 signatures. Early in October 2005, the Lord Advocate, on behalf of the Crown, did lodge an appeal, claiming that the sentence was too lenient. The family's petition was calling for a ten-year sentence. On 20 October, the appeal was heard by three High Court judges and, a fortnight later, Carol McMillan was sentenced to four years in jail for the vicious attack on Ann Whittle. Most would observe that it was no more than she deserved. Incidentally, at his trial, her partner Freeburn had his sentence deferred for six months for good behaviour. He complied with the court order and was then admonished.

The family cheered the appeal court verdict and, with McMillan finally behind bars, the papers reported that Norman Whittle, whose wife it turned out had had an undiagnosed heart condition, said it was a result he had prayed for. He said, 'I burst out crying, thinking of my wife. I am just so happy today. We deserved justice.'

At the appeal, Lord Cullen, who sat with two other judges, said, 'There is no reasonable alternative to a custodial sentence.' As he spoke, McMillan sat hunched in the dock.

Brian McConnachie QC had told the appeal:

The position of the Crown is that the circumstances of the offence were such that there was no sentence which could be imposed other than a substantial cus-todial sentence. It was an assault in which a signifi-cant level of violence was used, involving pulling of the victim's hair and kicking her on the head while, to all intents and purposes, she was on the ground and helpless.

While the victim was literally dying in the street, McMillan went on the phone, while sitting on the bonnet of Mr Whittle's car, telephoning the police and claiming that she was being assaulted by Mr Whittle with his vehicle and that she was the one who had been the victim of an attack. It is clear, at the time these injuries were inflicted, there was no hint of remorse from McMillan.

Mr McConnachie went on to say that the sentencing judge, Lady Dorrian, had taken McMillan's personal circumstances into account too much – although it was not disclosed exactly what those circumstances were.

It was not the first time decisions of Lady Dorrian had been questioned. In the summer of 2006, as this book was being written, I allowed myself a wry smile when I came upon a national newspaper featuring a story 'naming and shaming' a number of judges for what were considered inappropriate sentences. On the list was Lady Dorrian. As I said, I had been approached by the Whittle family to help in their dealings with the Criminal Injuries Compensation Board and thankfully that matter is being resolved with the assistance of the detective in charge of the original case, Detective Inspector David Gemmill. But the bottom line is that the family of Ann Whittle have been taken to hell and back by the actions of the 'Woman Who Nearly Got Away with It'.

10

THE VAN THAT NEVER WAS

The police are often accused of paying too much attention to detail, the ritual of following procedures taking precedence above all else. But anyone who has pulled on the blue uniform and patrolled dangerous streets will tell you that sometimes procedures can save lives and that there is often a good reason for doing things by the book rather than reacting intuitively. I learned that lesson, often the hard way, on the streets of Glasgow on Friday and Saturday nights back in the sixties. The schemes were tough and so was the city centre. Sauchiehall Street, in particular, was no place to be late on a Saturday evening unless you were tooled up and a fully paid-up member of the Maryhill Fleet or the Roystonhill Shamrock. Strange as it may seem, in these days of pedestrianisation and city-centre gentrification, these two gangs often met 'by appointment' for a dust-up in the area of the old Locarno ballroom. Where there are now new luxury flats, blood was spilled on the streets with alarming regularity in those bad old days.

There were laid-down procedures for the guidance of police officers called in to separate street fighting gangs.

I have often heard laymen and -women complain that the use of the siren on a squad car simply warns the bad guys that you are on your way and allows them to escape. To some extent this is true but tackling gangs of thugs, whose main aim in life is to knock hell out of each other with razors, staves, stones or chains, requires a special approach We were always taught that, when called to a scene where there could be literally hundreds of combatants in bloody action, the sound of the siren screaming loudly through the night air helped stop the fight and made the street armies scatter. This saved lives and serious injuries – even if, on occasion, it let a villain or two escape.

In those days, the first stop after attending city-centre incidents was usually the casualty department in the Royal Infirmary – one of the busiest emergency medical facilities in Britain on Fridays and Saturdays at the time! – to check on the injured. It was important to find out if anyone had died as what might have just been a street rumble could turn into a murder inquiry. Gang fights give the police many problems but the most difficult of all was trying to prove, after the event, who had hit whom and who had thrown what at whom – in other words, to differentiate between attacker and attacked. It always was and always will be a minefield.

The history of true crime is riddled with illustrations of the problem. Almost eighty years ago, the death of one of the thirties' gang leaders highlighted the difficulty. James Dalziel was the ruler of a south-side gang known as the Parlour Boys who were based in a local dance hall. Then, as now, dance halls could be the focus of trouble with rival gangs fighting over the choicest of the local girls who would be decked out in their finery and on the pull. Often the men would have poured out of the local spit-and-sawdust drinking dens blind drunk. Problems stemming from drug use were in the distant future but the illegal chemical route to nirvana had its forerunner in a simple excess of booze. After an affray one night in the Bedford Parlour Dance Hall, in Celtic Street, Dalziel – known to his fighting mates as Razzle Dazzle – ended up taking a trip to the nearby Victoria Infirmary, mortally injured, on the back of a lorry commandeered into use as a makeshift ambulance. He was dead on arrival and no fewer than sixteen men appeared in court accused of inflicting stab wounds or razor slashes.

At the height of this affray in the dance hall, women screamed and fled for cover as the men battled it out with razors, knives and bottles. After an intense weekend of police activity, sixteen of the dancers were arrested. The police operation involved one of the largest identity parades ever held in the city – or anywhere else, I suspect. Almost a hundred young men and women who had been at the dance took part in the line-up. When the accused, all in their twenties and thirties, finally appeared in court, most sported bloodstained bandages on their heads or bodies. The man suspected of delivering the killer blow somehow got the jury on his side and escaped the rope.

The whole business showed just how difficult it is to mete out justice after a gang fight and I had a similar experience myself in the sixties. The location was the old Locarno in Sauchiehall Street. At one time this a real hot spot and it was frequently visited by cops trying to sort out the bad guys from the folk just there for a night out and a twirl round the floor with the prospect of what Glaswegians call a 'lumber' at the end of the night.

Extra patrols were often at the ready to rush to an incident and, if something serious happened, the manager would be briefed to close the doors to make sure the combatants didn't do a runner. I well remember one night we arrived to sort out what was happening behind the doors the manager had locked. There were 200 male dancers in the hall. We propped the victim, who was bleeding profusely from his injuries, on a chair and put down towels to catch the blood before arranging for the dancers to file past, one by one, to let him try to finger the villain. Some hope with such a number of possible assailants! The injured guy was on the verge of passing out from his injuries when he managed to gather enough breath to tell us that the person who had chibbed him had red hair. Suddenly the suspect list had narrowed to eight people. That time, we got a result and the person responsible for this bloody attack got eight years but, if he had not had red hair, would we have caught him?

If gang fights as an indoor sport cause problems, those that take place outside can be an even bigger headache. Nothing much has changed in this since the twenties and thirties. Groups of youths still confront others with all sorts of weapons and sticks and stones as they defend what they call territory or try to move in on another group's area. In Glasgow, the defining line between one gang's patch and another's can be a main road and innocent motorists are at much risk passing through such places. Stones hurled from one 'war zone' to another across the street can hit cars and potentially lethal objects can be dropped from motorway overpasses.

It is all mindless stuff and, if you ask the gangs why they are fighting, the answer is often that the other lot have no right to come into 'our patch' or simply that 'we hate them'. I suspect much of it is just because there are neds who like a bloody battle.

The innocent do get hurt and a tragic case in which A Search for Justice played an important and successful role shows that in dramatic fashion. Gang fights over territory are not exclusively a Glasgow phenomenon – much of the wrongdoing that takes place there is mirrored in cities up and down the land. This one took place in Dundee and ended up with a demonstration that, if victims of injustice fight hard enough, they can make their point. Although this case ended up as a success on paper, the tragedy is that an innocent fifteen-year-old boy was dead.

On 30 March 1998, young John Kidd went out after his tea to indulge the usual teenage passion for football. He met a group of friends in Drumgeith Park and had a kick-around. This harmless burning up of energy in an attempt to mimic the heroes of the real-life clubs they supported ended dramatically. The young footballers were attacked by a gang known locally as the Fintry Shams, denizens of a tough local housing scheme. The time was around 9.45 p.m. and, in a way that is not unusual, neighbours near the park sensed trouble was in the air that chilly night. Calls were made to the police but, for one reason or another, no assistance came. In the meantime, John Kidd was hit in chest by a stone thrown by the invaders. This injury was so severe that it killed John.

A few minutes before the fatal blow had been struck, a police van had reportedly been seen going along Pitkerro Drive, one of the park's boundary roads, only a few yards from where John was to die. Reliable witnesses claim that they attempted to signal to the driver of police van and his companion to stop but the van simply went past on its way to whatever, wherever. As I have said earlier, the arrival of the police at a gang fight usually results in the fighting mob scarpering as soon as they see a blue light or hear a siren. Had this van stopped and the officers taken an interest, it is my view that the Fintry Shams would have taken to the hills and John Kidd would still be alive.

Hearing of the disturbance and worried about what was going on, John's mother ran towards the park. Meantime, friends and neighbours were trying to comfort the injured boy as he lay on the ground. A few minutes later, an ambulance and, belatedly, several police cars arrived. The paramedics were swift to realise that the boy was dangerously injured and reported back to base on the extent of the emergency and the cops, too, were quick to act. They intercepted Mrs Kidd as she made her way to the park and, instead of letting her travel to the hospital with her dying son, they drove her to a local police station where she was interviewed. Almost an hour later, she was taken to the hospital. When she got there, she asked about her son and, without being told anything, she was taken to a cubicle. Pulling aside the cubicle's curtain, she found her son lying there dead.

An arrest was made but, in court, the case was found not proven and the accused walked free. This family tragedy was becoming more and more horrific.

Through their solicitor, the Kidds questioned the behaviour of the police on the fateful night. In particular, they wanted to know what the police response to the neighbours' phone calls reporting the gang fight had been. They were told that a detective constable had acknowledged a radio message about the calls but that he had failed to attend the scene. This officer was suspended for a period of nine months. Astonishingly, one explanation given to the family was that he had acknowledged the call but 'forgot to attend'.

So now we come to the mystery of the van which reliable folk said they had seen go past the park. The family's initial questions on this were met by an answer to the effect that such a van could not be identified. And, on 8 April 1999, they received a letter from the Tayside Police which said, 'The matter of the passing police van regrettably still remains unsolved though I am advised that it was dark at the time.' The outside observer could be forgiven for supposing that the whereabouts of a police van at any given time would be known.

It was in August 2002 that the family turned to A Search for Justice for help. They believed that they were being given the run-around and it is difficult not to agree that, regrettably, this seemed to be the case. We are back to the issue of following procedure with which I began this chapter – in this, case the basics were not followed. Incidentally, before we got involved, there had been another meeting between the family and the police, in June 2000, during which a superintendent candidly told them that, if the officer who had originally been contacted *had* attended the incident, 'there is no doubt that your son may (*sic*) still be alive'.

A Search for Justice discussed the case at length and it was agreed that I should travel to Dundee to meet the family and this I did. I visited the location where the attack had happened, took photographs and interviewed witnesses. When we went to the scene of the tragedy, one witness proved particularly helpful. He graphically demonstrated his actions on the approach of the van and his attempts to force it to stop. His re-creation of the events was so realistic that, at one point, he almost got himself knocked down. Asked if he had made eye contact with the driver, he insisted he had and that the driver had also seen him but, when we spoke to the police, I was told by a female superintendent that 'there was no police van in the area at that time'.

Search for Justice took a report I had produced to the family's solicitor. The upshot was that I was precognosed, in Edinburgh by counsel representing the family. In dealing with legal matters and in the courts generally, you can never be sure of an outcome to any action and, at one stage, this looked as if it could go either way. However, I stuck to my interpretation and the belief that, if the police had acted correctly and according to procedures, it was possible that John Kidd might not have died.

It ended up as a major success for the Kidd family and their legal representative. Eventually, Tayside Police admitted responsibility and agreed to pay compensation but some questions remained.

Much of the furore over this case had been stoked by various *Sunday Mail* investigations and reports – and rightly so. Their crime expert, Marion Scott, who had a long involvement with the case, got in touch with the family for what the papers call a 'wrap-up' piece and what emerged was astonishing. It seems that, when the detective constable received the call about the disturbance at the park, he was playing cards. Who with? Only one policeman was disciplined. Where were the officers in charge of the station? Could it be that the mystery officers in the mystery van were also playing cards? It is a sad episode. And no part of it is sadder than the fact that poor John Kidd died alone in the ambulance when his mother could have been holding his hand as he passed away . . .

11

AN ARMCHAIR, A FILM ON TV AND A DOG

When fleeing bank robbers are caught on film and TV, it usually involves a street chase with squad cars being driven like F1 racing cars. There are tyres squealing and sirens blaring out as the cops go in hot pursuit of the bad guys. After a series of sensational shots of near collisions, much skidding around and handbrake turns worthy of rally driver Colin McRae, the robbers are eventually pulled over and arrested. Reality is often very different from this. It certainly was in the case of a guy who did a bank in the centre of Glasgow.

As I was passing an idle moment or two playing table tennis in the station with Detective Constable Joe Woods, we were interrupted. The police radio was barking out an urgent appeal for a squad car to go to a bank in Hope Street where there had been an armed robbery. It wasn't quite on our patch but the response to this appeal seemed to be a little tardy so we stopped the big ping-pong battle and headed for the scene.

Uniformed officers had arrived a minute or two before us and we all found the staff in a state of considerable shock. The manager told us what had happened. A fairly respectable-looking man had walked in and asked a teller to arrange for him to have a word with the boss. It was done there and then and the manager, thinking he was dealing with a prospective customer looking for a loan, got a real surprise when the visitor pulled out a gun and ordered him to call the cashier into the office. You don't argue with a guy waving what you believe to be a loaded handgun in your face and the manager quickly complied.

The cashier was told to get £5000 fast, which she did. The raider carried a holdall – which might have been a clue to his intentions – stuffed the readies into it and beat it out on to the street. Fortunately, one brave young teller had the presence of mind to follow him and saw him disappear into reception area of an office block not far from the bank. The teller quickly took us to where he had seen the robber disappear.

We got a dog and a handler and I told the dog branch man to stand at the main door to this bolthole and let no one in or out. Joe and I then started a search of the building starting on the ground floor and working upwards. In a third-floor toilet, we found an imitation gun, a sports jacket and a small tin of face cleansing pads. This tin had a label attached to it indicating the chemist who had sold it and the address was of a shop in Currie, a fairly nondescript little town to the west of Edinburgh.

I wondered why this particular floor in a large building had been used to dump the stuff and we got a lead when we discovered that on the same floor was a hairdresser. It was no ordinary cut and trim place but an upmarket business specialising in customers who wore toupees.

And it was the sort of establishment where you made an appointment. Yes, a few minutes after the robbery had taken place, a customer from Currie had popped in for a trim. The danger of vanity!

The young girl who had attended him was helpful. While at work wielding the scissors, she said she had heard the sound of police sirens nearby. She also noticed the customer had traces of 'grease' on his face, that he was sweating heavily and that he had a holdall which he kept tightly clamped between his feet. The guy was a regular and the girl knew him but normally he was so tight with his money that he never tipped. He did this time and little wonder with £5k in his holdall. It did not take a genius to figure out that the man in the toupee would turn out to be the bank robber. By the time we had discovered this, our boss in the CID had arrived. We told him what had transpired and, of course, he suggested we head out east on the motorway towards the capital and get to the address in Currie as soon as possible. He added that we should take the police dog with us to help identify the robber. I asked if the dog would bark, growl, wag his tail or just bite the suspect. We went without the dog!

We set off at high speed for Currie. We found the house without much bother, knocked on the door and were admitted by a young woman, who told us her husband was in Glasgow 'on business'. He returned half an hour later to find two detectives sitting, quite at home, in his armchairs watching a Jeff Chandler movie on TV and drinking tea. The wife indicated us and said, 'These gentlemen want to speak to you.'

'Can I help?' he said and we informed him that we were here to arrest him for a bank robbery carried out in Glasgow earlier that day. He immediately passed out in a faint and had to be carried over to a sofa.

When he came to, he blurted out the whole pathetic little tale. He had a business that was experiencing cash-flow trouble and the Edinburgh banks would not give him the money he needed to sort it out. In desperation, he decided to help himself from a Glasgow bank. He could see no other way out. He told us he had scouted the bank in Hope Street the week before the raid and that he was in the city for his monthly trim on the day of the robbery. He confirmed what the bank manager had told us and said that, when he had left the hairdresser and gone down to the street, he was confronted with a policeman and a dog. He said he had patted the dog which wagged his tail for him. Maybe the boss was right and we should have taken the dog to Currie!

The guy was no desperado. The gun was an imitation one though it was realistic enough to scare the bank manager. He had had no previous dealings with the police and had clearly been driven to the robbery simply by the worry of his business going down. He was desperate for us to tell him what would happen to him and we suggested, taking his background into account that he would be dealt with in reasonably lenient manner. Indeed, we told him we thought that three years might be par for the course.

He pleaded guilty at the High Court but, yet again, we got a lesson on the dangers of trying to guess what will happen in any court. You just never know. The week before the man in the toupee appeared in court, there had been a number of much more serious bank robberies in the city and, in one, a member of staff had been injured. The papers were full of it. The judge told our man that there was too much of this sort of thing going on and he was determined to crack down on bank robbery. He gave the raider seven years which, in those days, meant four years and eight months. I could not help feeling a wee bit sorry for our man. After all he had gone home, having got clean away with a bank robbery, to find two cops sitting in his front room.

The man in the toupee was a bit of a born loser, I suspect. But life can turn up winners as well, even if you are a cop. I have often chanced my luck in hard cases and got a result. But only once did I back a string of winners. Gambling on horses is not my scene at all – I was pretty sure that winning some cash was not a decent prospect. But there is always an exception and once, along with some colleagues, I did make a modest bob or two from a four-legged friend though in this case the assistance came from a dodgy two-legged character.

In the CID, you don't get much respite from chasing murderers in a city like Glasgow – especially when, even in the twenty-first century, it can still be called the murder capital of Europe. However, just occasionally, you do get a break from it and we were enjoying one such unusual spell of non-violence when the city's detectives got a call for assistance. It came from officers in Irvine down on the Ayrshire coast and they phoned at just the right time because, for once, we did have the manpower to be able to offer some help – something that doesn't often happen in Glasgow.

The problem was at the town's famous Marymass Festival. This popular annual event has a long history and thousands come to watch the street parade, which is led by the local beauty who has been chosen as that year's Marymass Queen. Most towns in southern Scotland have similar fetes and folk flock to them for all the fun of the fair but such gatherings also attract those who prefer to pick pockets and snatch handbags rather than ride a carousel or throw balls at coconuts to try to win a cuddly toy.

Anyway, when the Ayrshire cops phoned for assistance on this big day, I had to ask if they were sure it was really us they required and not traffic guys or beat cops – this was the Serious Crime Squad they were contacting, I reminded them. I was assured we were required.

It seems that, at the previous year's festival, there had been trouble at the 'horse racing'. This was news to us but it was explained that, as part of the festivities, horse races were held on a piece of open ground just outside town. This was not Ascot or York and it was certainly no glittering Jockey Club event with tiered grandstands packed with champagne-swilling toffs parading their finery. This was Ayrshire working folk having fun and spending their hard-earned cash – lots of it.

Two of the preliminary races were for the magnificent working Clydesdales that are such an attractive part of farming in these parts. They're not exactly the sort of animals that the Pony Express would use but they are extremely beautiful. However, the rest of the races were, if not for thoroughbred racehorses, at least for horses that looked as if they could run a bit.

Six of us had gone down the coast that Saturday but we were not really needed. There was no sign of Glasgow pickpockets having descended en masse on Ayrshire – a team from Saracen in the north of the city had been expected – and there were no signs of crowd trouble. It was shaping up to be a nice afternoon off. We enjoyed a pleasant lunch and wandered round the temporary racecourse.

After the first race was run, an acquaintance I met informed me that he had been given access to the result of the races in advance by a friend. How often have we all heard that? Nonetheless, it was agreed that he would stand outside the committee tent and five minutes before the start of each race indicate, using his fingers, the number of the horse that was expected to win the race. This was intelligence that I had to share with my colleagues. And, just as the second race was about to start, my tipster indicated the number four, giving the plain-clothes cops time to put on a small wager with one of the many bookies from the city who had come down for the event. Number four duly won and this turned out to be a regular occurrence on that pleasant afternoon in the sun. The cops were turning a nice wee profit even though, at this stage, it seemed as if the races were being run competitively.

The last race was a quite different affair. Our man Bert, as I will call him, promptly turned up outside the tent before the race and indicated we should back number five. The last race at any meeting always generates a lot of activity for the bookies – it's the last chance of the day for losers, ever hopeful of turning a profit, to chase their losses and, for the winners, it's a chance to use some of their winnings to make it an even better day.

The favourite for this last race was odds-on and carrying a whole bundle of money. At the start, this odds-on favourite's jockey was clearly seen to be having trouble positioning his mount and, not long after the field set off, the horse was already ten lengths behind. It had no chance and the eventual winner was none other than our number five. But the cops' nice little day out then turned sour as the crowd, suspecting a fix, became ugly. Everyone in the force there that day had a real job on their hands calming the unhappy punters down while making sure our winning betting slips were kept well out of sight!

12

Inside Job on an Inside Job!

Some detectives will tell you that, in this game, you are only as good as your informants and, to some extent, that is true. You can cut out a lot of time-consuming legwork on an enquiry if you have someone or other on the inside track. The only folk who keep a closer eye than the police on what's happening in the criminal world are the criminals themselves. And I know, from first-hand, that some criminals like to drop a titbit or two into the ear of a friendly cop if the result is a rival or competitor getting a few years behind bars. The anonymous tip-off is a good way of settling old scores without any need for messy violence or complications. Everyone likes a nod in the right direction when faced with a tricky case. In my time as an investigator, such 'steps for a hint', as cops would say, happened all the time and, like my colleagues, I cultivated a few criminals who enjoyed a bit of grassing if they thought it was in their interest.

Career criminals value the inside job. They are on the look-out all the time for the bent bank clerk who will hand over a key, a cleaner who knows where the cash is or someone in a warehouse or shop able to do bit of creative paperwork to disguise some thieving. And, if the thieves are clever, it can take months for what is going on to be recognised. That's where the annual stocktaking can come in handy. The usual culprit turned up by stocktaking tends to be a pub manager or a lowly employee in a booze bottling plant. But, on occasion, items a tad larger and less easy to conceal than a bottle of hooch are involved. I was once given an enquiry to track down a large number of bathroom suites that turned out to be missing when a plumbers' supply business did the annual check.

I spoke to the owner of the firm, a large and successful one, and he agreed with the police plan to do what you might call a reverse inside job. The bathroom suites were not walking out the window so there was only one explanation – an inside job. So we leaned on an ex-con who was conveniently out of a job and he was employed by the firm to fill an existing vacancy and secretly briefed to keep an eye on his workmates. The boss of the firm was so anxious to stop this business of the vanishing suites that he agreed to pay the spy out of his own pocket. Looking back, it all seems a bit of a no-brainer as they say nowadays. For a week all was quiet. Then I got a call from our man. He said that a lorry was heading out of the depot with two expensive bathroom suites and there was fake paperwork to cover them.

Our informant described the lorry, gave us the registration number and told us it was heading for Hillington Industrial Estate. We intercepted it, watched as some deliveries were made and then saw it go from Hillington towards Cathcart. We surmised that there would still be a bathroom suite left in the vehicle but it soon became obvious the driver knew he was being followed. An old trick I learned in my days driving Jags for the traffic department was to try to get a look at the rear-view mirror of any car you were following. Seeing the driver's eyes in it will often reveal whether he knows he has a tail and I reckoned this guy had clocked us. So we stopped the lorry and the driver confirmed he had spotted us following him. I told him we had reasonable ground to believe he was transporting stolen goods. He, of course, denied it. But we searched the cab to make it look good before we turned our attention to the bathroom suite which we were pretty sure was in the back. The driver produced a delivery note for a customer in Hillington, the area we had just left.

I ran an eye over the paperwork and said that someone must have given us a bum steer but added that we would escort him back to Hillington to let him make up lost time on the delivery. He insisted he was fine but I was adamant that a police escort would smooth the journey to the delivery point. When he finally realised we really meant it, he said, 'It's not going to Hillington – it's going to a house in Cathcart Road, Govanhill.'

We went with him to the address and knocked on the door, which was answered by middle-aged man. 'Bathroom suite?' I said and the man said, 'Just bring it in.' I had a better idea and just barged in. The phrase 'Aladdin's cave' is a bit overused but it describes exactly what we found.

We spotted three complete bathroom suites and many other valuable items of plumbing equipment. The driver and the owner of the flat were locked up and, while they languished behind bars, we paid a visit to their homes and it was no surprise to find they both had show-house style bathrooms. We then nabbed some of the warehouse staff and got some idea of where the stuff had been going. The bathroom furnishings were of high quality and our enquiries took us to a selection of wealthy suburbs where we found identical bathrooms, all recently acquired. It seems that, when offered a bargain, even high earners can't resist something that has obviously fallen off the proverbial lorry. One example of this was particularly revealing. It was in a leafy upmarket part of Pollokshields and the owner was a high-ranking naval man. He got on his high horse and insisted that it was not stolen property but then shot himself in the foot by admitting he had bought it in a pub.

All the suites we located in private houses were photographed and the 'owners' were interviewed. They were then all billed for the true cost by the firm from which they had been stolen and every one of them paid up. Our own inside-job man was offered a permanent position but he declined it. The case had taken a lot of police time and, during this, I became friendly with the owner of the plumbers' merchants, a man called McGregor who was amusing company with a fund of good stories. He was fond of classical music and one of his favourite anecdotes concerned one of his birthdays. He got a phone call at his city home and, when he answered it, the line was silent. He then heard James Galway playing 'Happy Birthday to You' on the flute. McGregor said to Galway, 'I thought you were playing the Carnegie Hall this week'.

'I am,' said the maestro, 'it's the interval!'

They lorry driver in the case of the missing bathroom suites couldn't do much about our searching of his lorry but it can be a different matter entirely if, in the course of an enquiry, you have to search a house. However, a good detective can develop the knack of getting into houses when necessary, even without a warrant. It takes a bit of doing at times because crooks tend to know exactly when a warrant is required and when it is not. To them, this is a sort of insurance policy when they have something to hide and the bizzies are on their tail. Clearly, when the police need a warrant, they should have one but the procedures involved in obtaining a warrant can be time-consuming and can slow an investigation down long enough for the bad guys to have time to hide stolen goods or other pieces of evidence. And, naturally, the times a warrant is most needed tend to be out of hours, which presents an additional difficulty.

When I was a serving officer, if you had to, you could call out a fiscal or a sheriff to get one but it was not always the easiest of things to do. You could get a warrant from a justice of the peace but I usually felt that, if a case was going to end up in the Sheriff Court, then that is where the warrant should come from. So, in my flying squad days, I occasionally managed to get into a house without a warrant or without the express permission of the householder. But you had to be careful and I had one amusing case where you might say it was *me* who was the con man.

Detective Constables John Bekier and Brian McLaughlin were investigating a break-in at premises where a large number of cigarette lighters and other items had been pinched. The boys had a tip-off that the stuff was in a house in Overnewton Square and they asked me to help on a visit to the place. We knocked at the door and it was opened by an elderly man who seemed to be on his guard from the start – as though he had had some dealings with the cops in the past. In any case, he was adamant that, if we did not have a search warrant, we were not coming in. The constables looked at me for guidance and I gently suggested to the man that he might prefer it if we didn't discuss his business at the door, where the neighbours might be earwigging on what was going on.

He then showed us into the living room and, when I noticed six adults of the dangerous-looking kind sitting there, my heart sank a little. The guy who opened the door was, by this time, in full flight telling his friends that we were detectives and we had the effrontery to believe we could search the place without a warrant. The six nodded their heads sagely – that was simply not on. The owner of the flat then proudly announced to the assembled throng that the Serious Crime Squad had tried the same thing on him the previous week and he had sent them packing.

However, he was not prepared for what happened next. I shook hands with him and remarked, 'It's a pleasure to meet someone who knows the law. You're correct – we can't search your house without a search warrant.'

Bekier and McLaughlin were as taken aback as he was. The householder then blurted out, 'You're not like these other bastards – you're quite a decent guy.' If I had surprised them before, my next statement shocked them. I said, 'You have let the side down. You are obviously not aware that, under Section 223 of the

Summary Jurisdiction (Scotland) Act of 1963, if you or a representative swear at a police officer on or above the rank of sergeant, that officer, by law, can search your house without a search warrant. Therefore, I am entitled to begin a search.' We found the stolen goods in a cupboard of the living room.

Next we left the house for the station with the prisoner in the back of the car and, during the drive, he told us the names of the persons who had done the actual break-in. He offered to show us where they stayed and, on the way there, he suddenly pointed at two teenagers and said, 'They did it – that's them!' We stopped the lads and arrested them and, by this time, the car was pretty crowded with the three cops squeezed into the front seats and the three villains in the back. One of the teenagers whispered to the householder, 'Did they have a warrant?' It was difficult to keep a straight face and a straight line in the road when he replied, 'They didn't need one – I swore at him and he's a sergeant.'

With all three locked up – the teenagers for the break-in and the householder for receiving stolen property – John Bekier set about preparing the case. The following morning, I went with him to the Sheriff Court. In those days, detectives reporting custody cases went to a room where there were around six procurators fiscal depute and handed over the papers that one or other of the fiscals would read. The system worked sweetly and problems were collectively worked out. Unfortunately, things have changed since these days and now some say it would be easier to get an audience with the Pope than a word with a Glasgow procurator fiscal depute.

The depute dealing with our case read over the report that Bekier and I had handed in and was pretty quick to ask if we had search warrant. Our 'No, sir' was met with a testy 'Why not?' I jumped in to explain that we hadn't needed one since the householder had sworn in my presence and, as he knew, that allowed me, as a sergeant, to search his house without a warrant. The depute said that he didn't know that was the case and I took the papers to the registry where they were logged in. Back in the car, I suggested we just sat where we were for a bit, listening to the police radio. I suspected I knew what was about to the happen. Sure enough within minutes the call came – 'Detective Sergeant Brown to return immediately to the Sheriff Court and report to Mr Herron.' This meant big trouble – Henry Herron was the procurator fiscal for Glasgow and a genuine legend in legal circles.

He was stern faced as he handed me a law book and said, 'Show me where it says you can search a house if you are sworn at.' Things were getting really serious. I had to admit it wasn't in there and Mr Herron said, 'I know that!' but then, showing a flicker of humanity, he added, 'If you can tell me what the section of the act you quoted refers to, I will not, on this occasion, report you to the chief constable.' I was able to say to this man with encyclopaedic knowledge of the law that the section gives a sheriff the power to order forfeiture of housebreaking implements. His face was a picture. 'How did you know that?' he demanded and I told him I had asked Joe Beltrami (the legendary Sage of West Nile Street and one of the most famous defence lawyers in Glasgow's history) on the way up the stairs.

Henry Herron dismissed me with a motion of his hand and said, 'Don't slam the door on your way out.' I didn't.

13

DEATH UNDER THE WHEELS

One of the most famous of Glasgow murder cases was that of James Robertson, who was hanged in Barlinnie for the murder of his mistress. Robertson was a cop and, as I told in my book *Glasgow Crimefighter*, there was a strange link between us. As a newly qualified beat constable, I first walked the hard, dangerous streets of the Gorbals wearing the number D69 on my collar and the last cop to have had that particular identification had been Robertson. The real interest in the Robertson case was that it was an early use of a motorcar as a murder weapon.

James Robertson was a sad figure who could have escaped the gallows. He had driven his car over the prostrate body of his girlfriend in an attempt to make it look as if she had died as a result of a hit-and-run. And he could have got away with it if the investigating detectives had not been smart enough to spot, from the tyre marks and the damage to the body, that the car had moved back and forwards several times over the unfortunate woman. One of his defence team at the trial, the legendary Laurence Dowdall, believed that there

could have been a lesser charge or sentence if Robertson
had let the jury know the real nature of his affair.
Instead he chose to protect what he saw as his wife's
reputation and declined to acknowledge that this was a
crime of passion that had led to the death of a mistress.
Instead, he insisted that the victim had been a 'casual
acquaintance' rather than a lover and this condemned
him in the eyes of the jury as a truly cold-blooded killer
worthy of the rope. Before his walk to the gallows in the
Bar-L Hanging Shed, he even thanked Jock Cameron
and Manuel Kissen of his defence team and remarked, 'I
know I am going to hang in three or four days' time but
I am still glad I did not let my wife down in public.'

That Robertson was caught was a both a tribute to
vigilant cops and a demonstration of the difficulty in
investigating hit-and-run crimes. I had a close insight
into this in my own career with the tragic case of Sadie
Young. It happened back in the sixties in the bitter cold
of a January night on the windswept streets of the city.
Four youngsters went for a Chinese meal in Gordon
Street in the city centre and carefully parked and locked
their car, a Ford Cortina. Fifteen minutes later, a few
miles away in the Gorbals at Hospital Street, Sadie
Young and her nephew, five-year-old Stephen Ure, were
at a pedestrian crossing when they were mown down by
this same Cortina, which was now a stolen vehicle. On
impact, the car stopped momentarily. Young Stephen
had been thrown aside and was not seriously injured
but Sadie was under the car's driveshaft. The driver
immediately accelerated away and the car was last seen
being driven at high speed eastwards along Caledonia
Road. It was found abandoned in Braehead Street with

the mangled body of Sadie Young still trapped under the wheels.

I got a call at home and went as fast as I could to Gorbals Police Office to be briefed on what we knew about what had happened so far. Right away, there was an understandable complication. Senior officers were of the opinion that this matter could be handled by the traffic department but, as a detective, I took charge and decided to handle it as a murder enquiry. My reasoning was that, by driving off after the moment of impact, the driver of the stolen car deprived the victim of any chance of survival. Who knows what would have happened if an ambulance and prompt medical aid had been sought? Poor Sadie might have survived. I was much relieved later in the case when the procurator fiscal approved of my actions.

Having finished their Chinese meal, the owner of the car and his friends had, of course, returned to find the Cortina missing. They called the police and it was clear that they had no involvement in the death. The body of Sadie Young was first examined in the street where it was found. The injuries were as horrific as any I have seen in a long career and, after our initial look, the body was taken to the city mortuary. The car was taken to Helen Street Police Office for examination. We were determined to track down the cold-blooded killer who had driven for some considerable distance with a dying woman trapped under the car. The forensic team gave their best. In particular, they were looking for fingerprint evidence but there simply were no dabs available.

However, we did have one lead. After he had dumped the car, the driver had been seen running along a pathway on the south bank of the Clyde. Witnesses said he appeared to be carrying a blanket under his arm. We sent a support group to search the possible route of the running man and, sure enough, they discovered an old blanket that was still folded up. We got back to the owner of the Cortina who confirmed it had been in his car. This was all a bit worrying and the question arose of what the folded blanket might have concealed. Could it have been a gun?

This was no simple hit-and-run – it was turning into a major murder inquiry and we sought the help of the press. The Glasgow tabloids keep a daily check on crime because they know that the armchair detectives and true-crime aficionados will buy more papers if they contain juicy stories about those who break the law. But they do also help in the fight against crime. They freely run stories on the latest leads and appeals for information on what can sometimes be obscure complexities of particular cases. And often they turn up vital clues. The circumstances of Sadie's death made for real human interest and the papers were doing everything in their power to help our enquiry. My team from the Gorbals was joined by officers from the Serious Crime Squad and, at the briefing, I emphasised that we were looking for a murderer.

Detectives from 'A' Division concentrated their investigations on Gordon Street and the nearby area, including doing a careful check on the results of enquiries into cars stolen from the area. It was thorough work. We made door-to-door enquiries in houses both at the scene of the original accident and around the area where the car was found. We found one witness who had been walking in Caledonia Road and described a car driving past at speed and making a noise consistent with something being dragged underneath it. This witness claimed to be able to give a detailed description of the driver despite the fact that the interior of the car was in darkness. It didn't seem possible but, in our efforts to solve this horrific crime, we tried an experiment. I arranged for a detective who I did not know to drive a car at a fast speed along Caledonia Road in a recreation of what had happened when Sadie Young died. Along with Detective Superintendent Alex Sampson, I walked the route and waited for the cop car to hurtle past. When it did, neither of us had a 'Scooby', as they say, who the driver was. Our witness was either a fantasist or an optimist.

We had little to go on and soon realised the only way ahead was the sheer slogging hard work of turning over anything that could remotely help. We went to the extent of producing a list of all known car thieves on the south side and they got a knock at their doors. Every car that had been stolen from Gordon Street in the immediate past was traced and gone over forensically and, in particular, searched for fingerprints. Active criminals, bank robbers and the like, who were known to use stolen cars on jobs, were traced and interviewed. Even the most hardened criminals had been sickened by the details of Sadie's death and they helped us as much as they could – some even suggested the names of possible suspects.

There was an interesting sidebar to this aspect of the enquiry. We lifted one suggested suspect who had been fingered by the underworld and he was put into an identity parade but not picked out. However, a few weeks later, as part of another investigation, this guy took cops into a remote woodland in Aberdeenshire and pointed out the grave of a man he had murdered and whose body he had buried.

We kept the file on the death of Sadie Young open for a long, long time and we threw everything we had at it but no one was ever brought to book for her death. This was a hard case indeed – too hard for us to crack. But I had my theories. Many armed robbers were active in the south side at the time. The incident happened on a Sunday night. Was the Cortina stolen for use on a robbery at a post office or bank on the Monday morning? We arrested all the members of one particular gang in connection with an armed raid on a post office van in the Gorbals. This lot had a flat in the Dennistoun area and were responsible for several such robberies. Prior to each hit they had gone to the city centre to steal a car – the way they operated fitted a pattern. But they were no ordinary armed thugs – they were part of a paramilitary group with political leanings and their robberies had a political dimension. The stolen cash was to be used in attempts to overthrow the government. They were very dangerous people – something that was corroborated by the fact that no one ever grassed on them. The consequences would be too dangerous. However, after their arrest, they were found guilty of the raid on the post office van in the Gorbals and given long sentences.

Because of my theory, I interviewed the ringleader but it was a waste of time. He was not talking about hit and runs or indeed anything at all. On the day after his arrest, this guy attempted to jump through the court window. Only an alert escorting officer stopped him making it out on to the streets.

Car thefts, then as now, were appallingly frequent. Teenagers are often to blame and a frequent ploy was to nick a car and do a few speedy blasts cruising around seeking some old lady who looked as if she had a few dollars in her handbag, snatch the bag and then disappear into the distance in the stolen motor. I remember one such incident well. This time we took the stolen car back to the scene and set up a roadblock. Every motorist who passed through at the material time was stopped and interviewed. We created massive tailbacks but, when Joe Public learned of the cause of the delay, they had no complaints. 'Catch the bastards!' was the most common comment.

This sort of stop-and-search exercise can produce some surprises. The massive one during the search for Sadie's killer uncovered numerous incidences of stolen cars in the city. One thief admitted having stolen around fifty cars in the previous six months – two a week. Another was 'motoringly challenged' as he told us he could not drive a car with a manual gearshift but he had still managed to steal twenty vehicles from the city centre! We got all sorts of strange tales. One guy said he had been a passenger in a stolen car when it was in a collision. Naturally, in these far off days, he was not wearing his seat belt and he went through the windscreen headfirst into the front garden of a house. His driver had not hung around after the crash and the passenger had lain unconscious for hours before he was discovered. We had to check this one out and we got another surprise. What he had told us was true and we discovered that a female passenger in the other car had died as a result of the collision. We arrested him on the spot and then handed him over to the division concerned.

Hit-and-runs are, sadly, too common but, at one stage in the Sadie Young case, it almost became a strange case of 'hit-and-tell' rather than hit-and-run. A suspect, a well-built youth around six feet tall and sporting a heavy growth of beard, had been brought into the office. He looked at least eighteen but turned out to be fourteen. He said he was the driver of the hit-and-run car. We were immediately suspicious. We grilled him on his story and it wasn't long before we could pick holes in his claim – he simply did not know the details of the crime. After a while, he gave in and told us that he was anxious to help us solve the crime. He was some talker and his next tale was to the effect that he had stolen a van-load of furniture from the Govanhill area and taken it to Easterhouse where he had given it to a priest as a gift, no doubt for distribution to the poor or whatever. This time he was telling the truth. The owners of the van and the furniture were reunited with their property and the priest got a word in his ear about accepting such gifts from fourteen-year-olds.

This youngster was obviously at the start of a career in crime and I remembered him a couple of years later. A girl had been raped at knifepoint and when she described her young attacker – now apparently six-feet-four tall – I remembered the would-be hit-and-run driver. We put him into an identify parade and he was picked out, locked up and sent to a young offenders' institution. At least that was a success but it still rankles with me that our fourteen weeks of relentless grind, all the door knocking, all the searches and all the road traps, had not uncovered the monster who drove a car with a horribly injured and dying woman trapped underneath it around the streets of Glasgow.

14

THE BODY BEHIND THE DOOR

When a detective looks back on a life of crime fighting, it is natural that the hard cases, the big mysteries, the complex investigations, the times when the head hits the brick wall, are those that are remembered best. Easy cases? Yes, I encountered some in my many years in the police and other investigative organisations but not many. Crime is seldom simple and the harder the case, the more impact it makes on your life. Some can actually change it completely and that's what happened with my involvement in the hunt to find the truth about the death of old Annie Davies, a hunt that was a turning point in my life. It was to draw me into years of private detection with A Search for Justice. During those years I tried to bring some mental peace to victims of violent crime.

Like many a life-changing moment, it started with a phone ringing and, as is often the case with interesting calls, this one came from a reporter – Marion Scott of the *Sunday Mail*. Down the years, the paper has kept a close and efficient watch on the criminal goings-on in Glasgow, a city whose crime scene is as active now as it has ever been. The date of the fateful call was 8 March 2002. For years, the *Mail* had been taking an interest in the suspicious death of eighty-three-year-old Annie Davies. Now they wanted my help and Marion asked me to contact old Annie's son, Bryan, at Erskine.

I was aware of background to the case, as were the many thousands of the *Mail*'s readers who followed the story. Old Annie had been found dead behind her front door at the foot of a steep staircase on 30 May 1998. The discovery was made on a Saturday, not the best of days to get the assistance of top policemen. Crime and crime fighting are round-the-clock operations but the cops are only human and, later in the story of the strange death of Annie Davies, I speculate what effect the day of her death had on the investigation.

As the *Mail* had asked, I visited the Davies Family and met Bryan and his wife Lesley. After the usual introductory remarks from both sides, we got down to business. According to Bryan, the police had come to the conclusion, right from the start, that Annie had lost her balance when going down the stairs and fallen heavily. This had led to her choking to death on her dentures.

Bryan went on to explain that, on the day of the discovery of her death, Annie's postman was doing his rounds as usual at 7.30 a.m. when he noticed Annie's door was slightly ajar, held open in that position by a pair of specs which were folded, not open. Postmen and milkmen are not strangers to unusual sights on doorsteps but the postie admitted later that he had seen many a thing behind or around doors but never a door held open by a pair of closed specs. However, he didn't open the door any further and it was late afternoon before the body was discovered.

A next-door neighbour, whose front door shared the same foyer, noticed the specs jamming the door and pushed it open to find the horrifying sight of the eighty-four-year-old lying dead. The neighbour picked up the specs, climbed the stairs to Annie's flat and telephoned an ambulance and also put a call through to Bryan and Lesley. The paramedics and Bryan and Lesley arrived almost simultaneously and it was perhaps fortunate that it was almost dark by now and the family was spared the full horror of the terrible injuries to Annie's face.

Soon after, two uniformed cops, a detective sergeant and a woman detective constable, arrived. The ambulance crew confirmed to them that old Annie was dead. The detective sergeant told Bryan, 'Your mother has fallen downstairs.' and went on with the routine ritual of getting family details etc. into his notebook. On 1 June, Bryan and his brother Fred, who had travelled up from England, were given back the keys of the house. It is of some significance that these keys were a spare set held by Bryan in case of an emergency. To this day, Annie's own keys have never been found. During the sad and emotional task of looking round his late mother's house, Bryan discovered that not only were her keys not to be found, there was no sign of her handbag or purse.

The realisation that something was seriously amiss and that it was too pat to say the old lady had fallen down the stairs began to dawn on the two brothers. Annie often carried large sums in her bag or purse, something that was known to local folk. And there is the fact that, when she went to the local shops and paid for her shopping, it would be easy for folk to see that the old lady had quite a bit of cash on her. By checking back from the entries in her bankbook, it could be calculated that she might have had around £2000 in cash in the house at the time of her death.

Like all detectives, I believe that little things can tell you a lot and, during my first meeting with the Davies Family, I was intrigued by the situation of the specs. If, as the police believed, Annie had fallen down the stairs, how had she managed to open the door? If she had been expecting a caller or had wanted to let somebody she knew in, she would have used the intercom at the top of the stairs to open the door. Right from the start, I suggested to her family that the more likely thing was that she had come down the stairs, holding the folded specs in one hand and using her free hand to grip the wall rail. This scenario had her opening the door and, just as she did so, someone on the outside kicked it in so hard that it smashed into her face, causing her to fall backwards with the specs spinning from her hand to land at the door. The assailant would then run upstairs, see the handbag or purse, which he may have known to be normally well stocked with readies, lift it and exit the house as swiftly as he could. The door had a spring to shut it and this could have led to the specs being pushed into the position in which they were found.

It was all a puzzle and it seemed like a good idea to go back to the house. There, with the permission of the new occupant, we experimented with the original specs, dropping them from various places and heights, but we never got them to finish up outside the door. There was another astonishing development – when you looked at the outside of the door from an oblique angle you could clearly see the outline of the heel of shoe on the paint at the appropriate height for someone kicking the door in. Remember this was four years after old Annie had died. I levelled with Bryan and told him that, at this stage, I strongly suspected his mother had been robbed and murdered.

On hearing this, Bryan remembered a strange conversation back at the time of the discovery of the body. He told me that, when a cop returned the keys of the house, he said, 'Your mother was murdered. We call it a run-through robbery.' He then pointed out that he didn't work for the division handling the case. I asked Bryan to describe the officer who had handed over the keys and he did, saying, 'He was about six foot four and looked like a film star.' In a moment of light relief, I figured he had just eliminated ninety-nine per cent of the members of Strathclyde Police Force. More seriously, later on, when Bryan was attempting to identify this officer, he was told by a senior officer that the description did not match anyone on the inquiry or in 'K' Division. On hearing this, I was a bit taken aback and drove to Barrhead Police Office in time to catch the back shift being briefed. The officer on duty gave me permission to speak to the guys and, when asked about this so-called tall cop with the Hollywood good looks, three people said they recognised the description and they all named the same person! He did exist but his observation did not significantly affect the case. I did not make contact with this officer – at this stage, it was enough to know who he was.

From the moment I first met him, one of Bryan's strongest complaints against the police was the accusation that proper procedures had not been carried out at the start of the investigation. I set about a paperwork search, reading all the various statements and reports I could get my hands on. This confirmed that I needed to speak to the authorities. I got an appointment with the regional procurator fiscal at Paisley.

I found him to be a man I could talk to and my first question hit the mark. I wanted to know who from his department had attended at the scene of Annie's death. I knew the answer already and he confirmed that the department had not been notified till the Monday though the death was discovered on a Saturday. Years of police work meant I knew fine well that Saturday is not the best of days to get the assistance of senior detectives. The detective chief inspector or detective inspector would be available but not necessarily in the police office. My imagination took me into a scenario. A detective sergeant would have phoned the DCI to report a death such as that of Annie. The DCI would ask if the officer thought it was necessary for him to attend the scene. If he was then told it looked like she fell down the stairs, he would then be quite likely to say, 'Let's see your report on Monday.' It could happen.

This hard case had been causing anguish to run through the family for years. Frustrated at the lack of information and progress over a long period of time, the Davies Clan had blitzed all sort of people and organisations with letters in which they set out their worries and complaints. During this time-consuming and tiring work, they sent letters to the police, the procurator fiscal, all sorts of folk in the media, MSPs and MPs. Much was promised as a result of this paper war but little achieved. The police offered some odd scenarios which, in my view, simply clouded the issues. For example, there was a claim that Annie was having trouble with her bifocals. According to the family, this was not true but it would explain why she was not wearing them as she went down the stairs. Anyone who wears specs will tell you that they often take them off going down stairs or escalators to allow them to judge the height of the step more accurately.

What was more important to me was the whereabouts of the money and her keys. I learned that, on the Tuesday following the death, a post-mortem was carried out at the city mortuary by Dr Alan Cromie and Dr Marjory Black, both of the university's department of forensic medicine. Each of them found that Annie's injuries were consistent with falling down the stairs but could not rule out a violent act. By the time I was on the case, Dr Cromie had returned to Ireland with his family for personal reasons but I spoke to him by phone. After we had discussed the injuries and how they might have been sustained, the doctor asked me why I thought it was murder rather than an accident. I told him all about the specs. 'What specs? I wasn't told about any specs,' he said. This was despite the fact that he had visited the scene and had been shown round the house by two officers. It was an unsettling conversation.

At a later date, I spoke to him again. This is part of our conversation:

Les Brown: Was this an accident or was it a
murder?
Dr Cromie: She was murdered
Les Brown: How was she murdered?
Dr Cromie: Exactly as you have described – struck
by the door.

A key move in the whole sad Annie Davies saga had
taken place in Belfast in 2003. Dr Cromie, armed with
documents and photographs, supplied by the procurator
fiscal in Paisley, held a seminar in a hotel attended by
forty medical colleagues. After all the presentations
and argument going to and fro among the assembled
experts, the conclusion was unanimous – all agreed that
the death of Annie Davies had been 'homicide'. This was
real progress and the media began to give new, serious
attention to what was turning into a major news story.

I had several meetings with the procurator fiscal at his
offices in Paisley and one of the outcomes was that he
travelled to Belfast to personally precognose Dr Cromie.
This was an unusual procedure and I could not recall
anything similar in twenty-six years with the police and
seventeen years with FACT. Normally, such statements
are gathered by what are known as precognition agents,
often police officers or retired police officers. The fact that
he had done the precognition himself was an indication
of how seriously the matter was viewed. I was interested
to learn that two detectives from Strathclyde had also
travelled to Belfast to precognose Dr Cromie.

The doctor called me after this to say he was unhappy
about the way he was questioned by the police. He said
their questions were all pre-prepared and that, just before

they left him, my name came into the conversation and one of the officers remarked, 'He works for the *Sunday Mail*.'

However, we were making progress of sorts. Dr Cromie came over to Glasgow and he and I went for a meal in a south-side hotel where we met the procurator fiscal for Paisley and discussed the case. He asked, 'You think this is a homicide, don't you?' The doctor said he did and I recollect that the procurator fiscal said that he did too. This was sensational stuff. After all these years, here was the regional procurator fiscal agreeing with me and the Davies Family that old Annie had been murdered.

We were now galloping ahead and the legal implications were moving up a notch or two. Next, Bryan Davies and I were asked to travel to Strathclyde Police headquarters for a meeting with an assistant chief constable (crime).

The start of our meeting was pleasant enough and we exchanged some shared memories but, from our point of view, the meeting was a disaster. He took us through the circumstances surrounding the death and told us that, in his opinion, old Annie 'did not have injuries to her face consistent with her having been struck by the door'. I could not believe what I was hearing. Realising we were wasting our time, I drew the meeting to a close by saying to the assistant chief, 'Why don't you look Bryan in the eye and apologise on behalf of Strathclyde Police for their mishandling of the case?' He replied that he could not do that.

Despite this negative meeting, we were still getting material to back up our belief about what really happened the day Annie died. On 18 May 2001 (a year before I came on board), Mr William Gilchrist, who, at that time, was the regional procurator fiscal at Paisley, wrote to the Davies family and said, 'I am satisfied that the circumstances of your mother's death are very highly suspicious and I have instructed Strathclyde Police that I do not think that this death should be described as accidental.'

This had been an extensive period of legal nit-picking. Many letters and documents had been exchanged and there had been several lengthy discussion meetings but then a new piece of information emerged to strengthen our beliefs. An acquaintance told Bryan that, a few days after Annie's death, his son had given him £2000 for safekeeping. The son was suspected by the folk in Erskine of being a drug dealer. However the police response to this was that they had interviewed the son and he had had a reasonable explanation for where the money came from. I wonder what that was!

But Bryan Davies was not easily put off. The urge to find out the facts of his mother's death had almost become an obsession. To illustrate the pressure he was under, I can point to a letter he received away back in the winter of 2000. The Crown Office wrote to him saying, 'The decision to take no further proceedings remains in place. Please do not seek to have this decision continually reviewed.' He was not to be pushed aside though and, three years to the day after the death, Bryan received a visit from three police officers.

Detective Superintendent Bert Dickov was leading a team taking a fresh look at the case. They went over all the old ground, all the old doubts and all the old evidence with the family and, out of it, came a glimmer of light at the end of the tunnel. The possibility of applying to Criminal Injuries Compensation Board (CICB) was raised. The cops pointed out that the conclusion of their inquiry was that the interpretation of the death was open to it not being an accident. This meant that making a claim was a legitimate thing to do. Bryan had never been driven to seek compensation – his motive was getting justice, not money – but, in light of the findings of the latest inquiry, it seemed like the right thing to do. He applied and the application was turned down.

He asked if I could find out why. It seemed that now almost everyone involved was agreeing that the death was 'very highly suspicious'. The one exception was the procurator fiscal who now appeared to have changed his opinion from the one that he had held when we had met over a meal with Dr Cromie. He had written to the CICB expressing a view that the death was accidental. I wrote to the Crown Office confirming our dismay at this outcome.

But, before this complex case was to move to a final outcome, there was to be another highly unusual series of events. During the Dickov investigation, Bryan had been asked if he owned a typewriter. He did not but the police fingerprinted every member of Bryan's family, including two grandchildren. DNA samples were also taken and, over a period of a couple of weeks, Fred, his brother, who lived in Lancashire, had twice been visited in his home by female officers. A third visit by three officers followed and then there was a fourth with four detectives, including Bert Dickov. Fingerprints and DNA were again taken. Considering it is said that getting a

DNA sample tested costs around £500 a time, this was turning into an expensive business. All that travel, too, must have been costly.

Back in Scotland, Marion Scott and a *Sunday Mail* photographer got the same treatment and tests. Obviously something serious had happened.

A Search for Justice never got to the bottom of all this. There is, however, a suspicion that, somewhere along the line, the police received an anonymous letter of some kind. This could explain the questioning about a typewriter. It is also a fact that DNA can be recovered from a stamp. It was an odd episode indeed but a clearer picture of what had happened was emerging.

During my initial investigation, I learned that the police surgeon who had attended the murder scene and had examined Annie's body was a Dr Gavin Watson, a medic know to me in my days in the CID. He was now a GP with a practice in Paisley and, when I visited him at his surgery, he remembered me. He confirmed he had been on duty on the day of the death and that he had been asked by the police to go to the house in Erskine. His job was simply to confirm that Annie was indeed dead and he did not immediately realise that she had serious injuries to her face. I asked if he had had any other connection with the case and he mentioned that, eighteen months or so before, he had been interviewed by two detectives, probably part of the Dickov team. I asked the doctor what they had wanted and he replied, 'Apparently money was missing from the house and it was to eliminate me as a suspect.'

This shocked me and I said, 'What on earth made you think that?' He said that the cops had asked him if he had looked round the house and, when he told them he had, they asked if he had been accompanied by a police officer! What nonsense.

We were at last reaching a conclusion and the Criminal Injuries Compensation Board agreed to another look at the case. On 28 June 2005, a full day's hearing heard evidence from the family, a member of the Dickov team and Dr Alan Cromie who had travelled over from Belfast to support the family. It all ended with a simple statement from the chairman of the panel to the effect that they had accepted that Annie Davies had died as a result of an act of violence and compensation would be paid. It was.

This remarkable story of a long and tortuous hunt for truth was the spark that started the now defunct A Search for Justice. It also played a role in the formation of Strathclyde Police's Cold Case Squad whose remit is to investigate unsolved murders. The long battle had proved worthwhile with one of the hardest of hard cases now being re-examined by the Cold Case Squad as a result of our efforts.

15

WHAT LIES BENEATH THE A9?

Football managers cover their backs in case of an unexpected defeat by trotting out, at every opportunity, the mantra that 'there are no easy games at any level'. It is not quite as bad as that in the detection game. There are murder investigations that almost solve themselves – cases where there is just one suspect and he or she has had both motive and opportunity and evidence against them is easy to find. It is also surprising how often a killer will start an interrogation with a vigorous denial of involvement and then suddenly, for no apparent reason, blurt out the truth. But, then, there are also cases, real hard cases, that remain unsolved for years despite the cops throwing everything at them. During such investigations, all leave is cancelled, uniformed officers are taken off other work to provide foot-slogging manpower for 'door to door' inquiries, the forensic experts are called in and there is massive help from the press and public. Yet what those footballer managers like to call a 'result' remains elusive.

Two cases, in particular, in my long career particularly spring to mind – the ongoing mystery of the Bible John murders in Glasgow in 1968 and 1969 and the mystery of what happened to Renee MacRae and her son Andrew in November 1976 up in the Highlands. In the first case no murderer or murderers have been found and, in the second, not only has the killer escaped detection but Renee MacRae's body and that of her young son are also still missing. I had some involvement in both these famous cases from the start and right up until 2006. One curious link to both cases is that, in all the years since they started making headlines, they frequently resurface in newspapers and television documentaries with new theories and sometimes new leads. But, at the moment, they are still unsolved murders.

The current thinking on Bible John is that he may not have existed and that the murders of Patricia Docker, Mima McDonald and Helen Puttock were not, after all, committed by the same man, as had previously been believed. At the peak of the investigation into what was thought to be serial killings of girls who liked a night out dancing at the Barrowland Ballroom in London Road, there was, however, no doubt in the minds of public or police that Bible John did exist. There was good reason for this since there was an apparent pattern to the killings. All the girls had been at the famous ballroom above the Barras market, all had been raped, strangled and their bodies dumped after they left the dance hall and there was a series of small, but significant, similarities to the modi operandi of the murders. And, at the time, it was felt no one other than the cops knew what these were and this meant the killings were not copycats.

Looking back, you can't be sure of that and the co-author of this book, Robert Jeffrey, has written extensively about his belief that, while two of the murders may have been the work of one man, there is reason to believe that one murder may have been committed by someone else. His theory – and I agree with it – is that the belief that the murders were the work of one person impaired the investigations of the second and third deaths and, if they had been investigated by different teams of detectives approaching each crime without baggage from previous investigations, they might have arrived at a different conclusion.

I was in on the Docker case, the first in the series of Barrowland murders, and made inquiries under Joe Beattie who ran all three investigations. However, our role in the Docker case was to eliminate one suspect from the inquiries. Joe and I had spent time together long before this (as I tell later in the chapter) and I find it of enormous significance that, before this legendary detective died, many years after the Bible John murders, he was publicly speculating that they were, maybe, not all down to the famous figure of Glasgow folk memory – the man in the identikit poster of a clean-cut sandy-haired young man with piercing eyes who the press had dubbed Bible John.

Later, I was involved when a guy who had been lifted on suspicion of being involved in one of the murders was released simply because he didn't fit the description of the serial killer in just one respect. In my opinion, he should have been investigated further. And other lines of enquiry into the murders of Mima McDonald and Helen Puttock were perhaps not followed up as strongly as they should have been because the people concerned did not seem to fit this Bible John creation.

Bible John scared legions of dancing daft Glaswegians away from the bright lights and big band swing of the ballrooms they loved. Police and public, at this time, all felt that they almost knew him. It was quite amazing and the city had a strange atmosphere about it for a period of three years or so. The impact of the hunt for the strangler on the public cannot be underestimated – during the furore surrounding the murders 50,000 people were interviewed and a hundred detectives were involved. The papers were filled with it day after day. Looking back, it seems we all seemed to know so much about the man called Bible John that maybe it led to folk – especially the police – not being able to see the wood for the trees, as they say. At one stage, Joe Beattie asked whether I would have done anything differently. I told him I would have gone on TV and appealed for women who may have been in Bible John's company and lived to tell the tale to come forward.

If Bible John did exist, he was a serial killer but not one in the same class as Peter Manuel who died on the Barlinnie gallows in 1958. Like Bible John, thirty-two-year-old Manuel killed for twisted sexual gratification. But the enduring mystery in his case is not about whether he was a killer – there's no doubt about that – but about how many he killed.

Scotland's most evil serial killer was actually born in New York in 1927 but came to Scotland when his family returned to Lanarkshire after a transitory spell in England. To anyone in the police at the time of his killing spree, the hunt for him was an endless source of speculation and conversation. He dominated the canteen talk in every police station in Glasgow. I was lucky enough to hear many an inside story of Manuel from Tom Goodall when, for a spell, one of my duties was to drive him around. Goodall, one of the best and best remembered of Glasgow's detectives, played a major role in sending Manuel to the gallows.

Everyone knew how dangerous Manuel could be. I had a bit of a scare myself when in the Gorbals in the late fifties. A car had been stolen from the home of the Smart family – the Smarts, Peter, wife Doris and young son Michael, who was only ten, were all slaughtered by Manuel – and it was found abandoned in Adelphi Street, on our patch. I was one of a team sent to secretly observe it in case the thief, possibly Manuel, returned. No one ever came back to the car and we heaved a collective sigh of relief. Had it been Peter Manuel and had he been carrying a gun, he would, no doubt, have tried to shoot his way out of an arrest. Goodall was always of the opinion that Manuel had killed outwith Scotland and that one victim had been Sydney Dunn, a taxi driver of Durham, but no charges were ever brought against him for this.

With Manuel free and the papers reporting the regular break-ins, attacks and murders that seemed to be his work, the city was in the grip of a remarkable attack of collective nervous tension. A sergeant in the traffic department told me of returning to his home in Dennistoun one night. Arriving at his top-floor flat, he heard a scream from a neighbour's house across the tenement landing. The copper smashed in the door with his boots and ran into the house just in time to get a look at an intruder scrambling through the kitchen window and shinning three floors down the rone pipe to the street. The sergeant was convinced the man he had seen was Peter Manuel but all the enquiries we mounted come to nothing.

In *Glasgow Crimefighter*, my previous book on my career, I told of a close relationship I had with the colourful bank robber Samuel 'Dandy' McKay. He used to meet me secretly to give me tip-offs – usually ones that would get some rival locked up for a bit. McKay had a lot of the old fashioned criminals' code of honour about him: robbing banks and the like was OK but knocking little old ladies on the head was not, so Manuel's penchant for breaking into houses and shooting men, women and children was definitely not Dandy's style.

In fact, along with other career criminals outraged by the serial killer's reign of terror, he was of great help to the police in the Manuel hunt. Like everyone else, Glasgow's sizeable criminal community wanted the killing to stop. McKay knew Manuel and often spoke to me about him. Dandy had a financial interest in a gaming place called the Gordon Club in Gordon Street, near Central Station, and Peter Manuel went there from time to time. Dandy McKay was quick to tell Tom Goodall that Peter Manuel was the serial killer who was costing the police and public such grief. I was also interested to hear first-hand from Dandy that Peter Manuel was the only man he had ever met who scared him. That is saying something for Dandy McKay was no soft touch, a quick thinking and physically strong hard man. He did not scare easily.

The Manuel inquiry had started out in Lanarkshire and there was concern that, although he was a stand-out suspect in the early murders, it was taking too long to nail him. Indeed, again with the assistance of that wonderful thing hindsight, there has been much serious criticism of the way the murder hunt was handled in the early cases. Goodall was moved on to the hunt when it seemed stalled and he was the man who was really responsible for catching the killer. Help from the likes of McKay and other clues turned up under Goodall would bring the serial killer to his fate.

After the Smart murders, a search of the home of Peter Manuel's parents found a distinctive type of lighter that had come from the Smarts' house. Many on the team hunting him thought that this was enough to lock Manuel up. That wily sleuth Tom Goodall had a better idea – lock up the parents. It was a masterstroke. With his parents now implicated, the killer gave himself up to Goodall and started to confess to his evildoing.

Manuel stood trial for eight killings and was convicted of seven. The one charge that did not stand up in the High Court of Glasgow was the murder of Anne Kneillands. In fact, the psychopath had confessed to killing this pretty young East Kilbride teenager but there was no corroborating evidence for the confession and the charge was dismissed. The actual trial of this fiend was one of the most heavily reported cases of the last century. As in the MacRae and Bible John cases, Manuel and his murderous career are regularly revisited by criminologists and there is now a consensus that he killed up to fifteen people.

Peter Manuel was a cool customer. It has been said that he ran to the gallows when he finally knew the game was up. He had defended himself in court and had faked mental illness all in a well-thought-out and desperate effort to escape the gallows. But, in the end, with all hope gone, he remained cool. Tom Goodall interviewed Peter Manuel in-depth in the death cell and questioned him about many unsolved murders without any success. He was even questioned about the Moira Anderson case. Tom Goodall told me that his last words on his way to the rope were, 'Turn up the wireless and I will give you no trouble.' An evil life ended seconds after that and the city struggled back to normality after years of fear.

As a detective, I was often embroiled in controversy so it is interesting for me now to see how this case is picked over in fine detail and how the police are regularly regarded as not having got the serial killer behind bars and at the end of a rope quickly enough. I will say it again – and it comes from the heart and long experience – hindsight is a fine thing. Some of that long experience was garnered in the company of Joe Beattie. Like Goodall, he was another legend who played such a pivotal role in the Bible John hunt.

Back in 1976, the year Renee MacRae went missing, I was sent on a course at the police college at Tulliallan, near Alloa. The course was intended for sergeants who seemed destined for higher things so to be there at all was a real privilege. I enjoyed it hugely. The college is housed in a converted castle. It is an impressive pile with huge halls and reception areas and acres of beautiful well-kept gardens to stroll in. During the Second World War, officers and men of the Polish Army were accommodated there and, for a time, it was a hospital.

Now, despite its age and its baronial feel, it is a place where would-be lawmen get a grounding in the job using high-tech aids like video recreations of high-speed chases and lessons in traffic police work. There is even a realistic bar area for the aspiring officers to act out scenarios like dealing with pub trouble and enforcing the licensing laws. And, for lovers of television whodunnits, there is a real bonus. One of the huge rooms has walls lined with books and in behind the shelves there is a secret door leading to a hidden cubbyhole – eat your heart out, Agatha Christie!

Right from my first visit I loved the place. We each had a room of our own and meals were taken gathered together in a huge dining room. On my course, there were thirty of us from forces around the country and we had all been talent-spotted and earmarked as destined for greater things. I knew most of the west of Scotland guys of course, but there were many officers from county forces who were strangers but who became friends and valuable contacts down the years of detective work that lay ahead.

The regime, however, was fairly strict and, at that time, the deputy commandant was the famous detective Joe Beattie who was to spend years on the tenement-lined streets of Glasgow. On that first visit to the college we had a enjoyable day of introductions and pleasantries before the hard grind started the next day. We were split into groups of ten and each group had an appointed class supervisor, a role that was filled by a different officer each day. I was at an immediate disadvantage. After each day's work, we had to write up a report and at night the chatter of old-fashioned manual typewriters echoed down the corridors. Unlike most of the guys from the county forces, I could not type. I went to the typing pool supervisor, a helpful woman, and explained the problem and she asked me to give her my reports on a tape and she would type them up. It worked like a dream though some of the guys – the ones who were destined to be *really* good detectives – were suspicious of the neatness of my reports and the lack of typewriter chatter from my room. I explained I had one of the latest state-of-the-art electric machines! I got away with it.

We had one grim shadow hanging over what was generally a good time in rural Clackmannanshire. On a day when I was designated the class supervisor, it was discovered that a sergeant from Glasgow was missing. The instructor that day was an inspector from Edinburgh and I explained to him that Sergeant X was unwell and I had told him to stay in his room. Wanting to save the missing man from getting into trouble, I left a note on his bed saying, 'You are ill – stay put.' On his late return to the college, he discovered the note. It turned out the delay had been caused by some domestic bother.

However, there was to be a truly tragic incident at the end of the course when the inspector from Edinburgh went missing himself. For some unknown reason, he had hurled himself to his death off the Forth Bridge.

I was still attending the course when the Renee MacRae story broke. The link was Donald McArthur, a sergeant from Inverness. We got up to some high jinks on that course and became good friends. However, one part of the course involved each of us giving a fifty-minute lecture to the assembled students. It wasn't too fearful a prospect for the Glasgow cops who were well used to giving evidence in court and standing up for themselves in public but the country cops were a bit scared by having to do it. You had to give a choice of three subjects and I boldly picked (a) the Battle of Bannockburn, (b) William Wallace and (c) the Loch Ness Monster. Donald found the choice less easy and, after suggesting (a) camping on Skye, followed by (b) around Skye on a canoe, he was stuck. I convinced him that (a) would certainly be chosen and said he might as well make (c) anything at all – something like the life and times of Joseph Stalin. He wasn't too sure but eventually agreed.

A week later I was told my choice (a) was requested. I always like to do a bit of research and visited museums and the like to gather notes on the battle. I was surprised to find that no artefacts have ever been found to confirm that what we now call the site was where the battle actually took place in 1314. In my opinion, the exact site had never been identified. People often accuse policemen of having no sense of humour but they had that day. In an effort to distract me as I spoke, members of the audience held up signs bearing legends so that I could see them but the instructor judging me could not. The least offensive of them simply said, 'crap'.

This section of the course had traditionally proved a bit of fun. At a previous course, Jim Binnie, who went on to head the CID in Glasgow, spoke on whales. He contrived to have an officer in the audience ask him which was the largest species of whale to which Jim would reply that is was the blue whale. But, instead, the questioner asked him about how the blue whale mates. Jim rose to the occasion. 'The participating whales, male and female,' he said, 'swim away from each other for a mile, turn and swim back towards at each other at speed. When they come together head-on, they rise out of the water and make sexual contact.' No wonder he got to the top.

Naturally, Donald was asked to pontificate on Stalin and, when he learned this, that's when I learned how a Highlander could swear. But, before he had had time to give his lecture, Donald was promoted to inspector and called north. His first job: to help in the investigation of the disappearance of Renee MacRae and her son, Andrew.

I was soon to head north myself on a visit to various police offices in the Northern Constabulary area to study what was on offer for officers in terms of sporting or leisure facilities and compare notes with other forces. I was teamed up with officers from Lothian and Borders and Central Scotland. My fellow officers on the trip decided to drive up overnight but I fancied a flight north the next morning. The plane was due in Inverness at 9.30 a.m. and getting to the police HQ in the Highland capital for the 10 a.m. start was going to be really tight. In fact, it was pretty well impossible even if the 'budgie' used on the Highland routes was on time and I was lucky enough to get a cab right away. The plane landed on time but, outside the airport, there was a long queue for taxis. As I waited my turn, a police car drew up and a uniformed cop got out and went to hand in a letter to the terminal. I nabbed him on his way out and told him I was a detective from Tulliallan and I had to be taken to HQ. I made it with minutes to spare, the siren screaming all the way. The chief constable asked us how we had travelled up and seemed impressed when I said on the nine-thirty flight.

Life up there was a bit different from the streets of the Gorbals or Castlemilk. In one remote office, we were given a welcoming dram – in a teacup! Even in country stations in the far north, the chink of ice on crystal early in the day would have raised a few eyebrows.

It was a nice little trip and it gave me one insight into a hard case you might not expect to find in a book like this – the Loch Ness Monster case. We had been given an official driver – the guy would have been the top wheels man in any gang. He could shift in a car and safely. He was impressive and it was interesting to hear him tell of seeing the monster while on duty. It was not something he spoke much about in public for fear of ridicule but, in a cop-to-cop natter, he told us he was sitting on the lochside when an animal rose out of the water close inshore. He told us it had 'the head of a giraffe, skin similar to a seal, huge round eyes and a long neck'. He was reluctant to call it the monster but insisted he had seen an animal as he described it. I was glad I was not on the case!

During the visit, the chief constable told me of a case of a young girl of four who had gone missing after a row between her parents. Apparently the child's home had been searched but there was no sign of her. Later that evening, traffic cops found the wee lassie in a car with her father and they were shocked to hear that, when the house had been searched, the girl had been hiding in a cupboard under the stairs. The chief told me that a senior man from Strathclyde was coming north to investigate this failure. I knew the officer and said that they should not expect too much help as I suspected this policeman would not have found her either. Searches can be a problem. I always told my guys to work on the assumption that what you were looking for was always there and that you will find it.

We returned to Tulliallan for the completion of the six-month course and the final part involved an interview with the commandant, an ex-military man who'd held a top rank. My pal Joe Beattie complimented me on my work during the course and gave me a hint for the final hurdle. 'Make a fuss of his dogs' was his advice. Sure enough, two beautiful golden Labs were present at the interview. I spent much time stroking them and telling them what fine fellows they were and they responded by swishing their large tails from side to side, almost sending ornaments and the like flying. Most of the interview then turned to a conversation about our mutual love of dogs and stories of my Alsatian, Rory. Joe thought I had done a good interview and done enough to pass out with flying colours. But the Labs played a role.

When I was back in Glasgow and busy with the serious crime squad, I got an intriguing call from Donald up in Inverness. The Renee MacRae case was taxing them to the limit – something we were well aware of because the case was big in the papers and on TV. Donald wanted advice and he had come to the right place as we were averaging a murder every five days at the time. Violent deaths and disappearances were everyday events in the city.

Donald ran over the details of the case. Renee and her husband, Gordon, were separated and they had two children, Andrew, aged three, and his older brother, also Gordon. Mr MacRae was a wealthy businessman. His company secretary, William McDowall, was supposedly having an affair with Renee and local gossip suggested that it was McDowall who was Andrew's father.

On the day that Andrew and Renee were last seen, Renee had told a close friend that she and McDowall were going to start a new life together and intended to meet in Perth. Renee drove a swanky and very noticeable BMW and, later that evening, the Beemer was seen ablaze in a lay-by ten miles south of Inverness. Neither Renee nor the boy was in the car and neither has been seen to this day. It doesn't take a genius to work out that this could have been the result of foul play. The police mounted a massive search of the area, including extensive visits to a nearby quarry called Dalmagarry.

Having listened to what Donald had to say, I suggested that he should speak to his chief constable personally and ask him to contact the chief in Glasgow and to see if he would be willing to put in a request for the serious crime squad, hopefully my team, to be sent north to assist.

That was thirty years ago and the debate about a national crime squad is still going on to this day – chief constables continue to resist letting outside experts on to their patches. The predictable answer to Donald's suggestion in the MacRae case was 'We don't need outside police forces to solve our crimes.' The answer might have been predictable but it was also wrong. The fact is that, if you are dealing with murder enquiries on a day-to-day basis, you are in a far better position to solve difficult cases than you are in a force where a couple of murders a year are the norm. But the fact that it is a clear no-brainer doesn't make it any easier to get it over to the smaller forces.

However, Donald and I still talked about the crime on a regular basis. The main problem was the lack of bodies and, as the old saying goes, 'no body – no murder'. The only slight lead came from witnesses who spoke of seeing a man dragging what looked like a dead sheep in the direction of the quarry. On the night she disappeared, Renee MacRae was wearing a jacket whose colour and texture could have resulted in the witnesses mistaking her for a dead sheep.

There were reasons for both the husband and the lover being suspects. And there was also the possibility that a hit man might have been involved. Such theories are not as far fetched as they seem. A search of the archives will show that there are people around who, for the right sum in readies, will take a life, cover up a murder and get away with it. But the stark fact remains that the police are no nearer to solving this thirty-year-old mystery.

A retired policeman, Sergeant John Cathcart, who was initially involved in the case and who has followed the twists and turns in the saga over the years, is convinced that the bodies are in the nearby quarry. He pushed his theories so hard that excavations were carried out and 40,000 tons of earth moved in the search for Renee and Andrew MacRae. Two top experts were there when this dig went on – forensic expert Susan Black from the University of Dundee and Professor John Hunter from the University of Birmingham. Both of them had assisted the Manchester Police in 2001 in the search for more victims of the Moors Murderers and Susan had assisted me in the Moira Anderson case.

John Cathcart based his belief on the fact that he had, in the early days of the investigation, smelled decomposing human flesh at the quarry. That is not a smell that you mistake or forget in a hurry – ask any murder squad man. But maybe, as that major search of the quarry seemed to suggest, the bodies were elsewhere.

Local farmer Brian McGregor was a man with a close interest in the case and, over the years, he had followed it, like Sergeant Cathcart and thousands of others, in the newspapers. His ground was near to where the burning BMW had been found. This gave him a special interest in the case and, for various reasons, he also did not see eye to eye with the Northern Constabulary. He conducted some amateur investigations of his own and discovered that workmen, returning to the site of the car fire on the A9 which was undergoing some reconstruction work at the time, claimed to have evidence that someone had interfered with the foundation rubble and infill preparatory to the tarmacadam being re-laid. Brian actually traced some of the workers and got confirmation from them of the exact location where this was supposed to have happened.

He was pretty convincing on the phone so I went north to visit him at his farm. If there is one thing that year after year of murder investigations does, it is to give you a pretty good understanding of witnesses – you can soon spot the phoneys and crackpots. Brian was a genuine guy.

Before we met, he had sought my advice on the phone on marking what he regarded as the suspect area on the A9 with a large yellow circle. I told him that, if he was determined to do it, he should do so in the dark as the local cops would arrest him if he did it during the day. He painted the circle and the local press photographed it.

Later we discussed whether there was anyway of finding out what lay beneath the circle without actually digging it up. I remembered seeing a radar device being used in Edinburgh that seemed to do just that. The machine looked like a large lawnmower. I suggested trying to get a university or a newspaper to give financial assistance in mounting a search with such a machine.

Then, on another visit to the farm in September 2006, I asked him how the underground search was going. He told me he had contacted a company in Dublin with expertise in this area. Two men with the appropriate equipment had travelled to the Highlands and he had guided them to the area he wanted searched. Here is what he had to say about the outcome: 'They found that there were three unexplained items under the road surface that were not consistent with the materials used to build the road.'

It had cost the farmer more than £1000 to have this search carried out. I told Brian McGregor that his investigation had now reached the stage where he needed to involve the police. If all this had nothing to do with the MacRaes, why would anyone interfere with the foundations of the road? What lay there now? In the category of Real Hard Cases, this one takes some beating.